T0022897

13-Digit ISBN: 978-1-40034-087-3
10-Digit ISBN: 1-40034-087-X

This book may be ordered by mail from the publisher. Please include $5.99 for postage and handling. Please support your local bookseller first!

Books published by Cider Mill Press Book Publishers are available at special discounts for bulk purchases in the United States by corporations, institutions, and other organizations. For more information, please contact the publisher.

Cider Mill Press Book Publishers
"Where good books are ready for press"
501 Nelson Place
Nashville, Tennessee 37214

cidermillpress.com

Typography: Adobe Caslon Pro, Festivo Letters No1,
Capriccio, Microbrew One, Trade Gothic LT Std
Illustrations by Rebecca Pry

Printed in the United States of America
24 25 26 27 28 VER 5 4 3 2 1
First Edition

TRUE
FACTS
THAT
SOUND
LIKE
Bull$#*t
WORLD HISTORY

500 PREPOSTEROUS FACTS THEY DEFINITELY DIDN'T TEACH YOU IN SCHOOL

SHANE CARLEY

CIDER MILL PRESS

BOOK PUBLISHERS

{ CONTENTS }

[Introduction]

If you're an American, you probably know a thing or two about the Founding Fathers. Who they were, what they did, and what they believed. But did you know that Thomas Jefferson wrote his own version of the Bible? Or that there were technically 14 presidents before George Washington? In *True Facts That Sound like Bull$#*t: World History*, you'll learn things your history teacher never taught you. Did you know that Hitler had a plan to kidnap the pope? Or that ketchup was originally sold as medicine? And did your teacher ever tell you about the time two nuclear bombs were dropped on North Carolina? Learn about all this and more, with 500 unbelievable facts from history's cutting-room floor.

The facts in this book run the gamut of history, from ancient Egyptian traditions to modern political scandals. You'll learn about eccentric emperors, unstoppable soldiers, and accidental inventions. You'll read about wars that lasted hundreds of years, and others that lasted just minutes. Some facts will make you laugh, while others will make you sad— but if you're interested in learning about some of history's most ridiculous people, events, and coincidences, this book is for you. With any luck, it will change the way you think about a historical figure or two!

Politics

There are plenty of colorful characters in politics today, and you need only turn on the news to see that the world isn't exactly run by the best and brightest. But would you believe that today's politicians are positively tame compared to the rulers of days gone by? Did you know that Napoleon's nephew tried to install a European king in Mexico? Or that a Dutch prime minister was once eaten by his own constituents? If you think politics is rough-and-tumble now, just wait until you hear what the kings and queens of old got up to.

1. USE OF THE GUILLOTINE DIDN'T STOP AFTER THE FRENCH REVOLUTION.

The guillotine was still the official method of execution in France until capital punishment was abolished in 1981. The device was used to execute a criminal as recently as 1977!

2. KING FREDERICK WILLIAM I OF PRUSSIA WAS AN EARLY DABBLER IN EUGENICS.

He attempted to breed the largest soldiers possible by forcing tall people to sleep together.

3. IN 1948, THE IDAHO DEPARTMENT OF FISH AND GAME DECIDED TO RELOCATE 76 BEAVERS TO THE REMOTE WILDERNESS IN THE CENTER OF THE STATE.

How did they go about it? By loading them into an airplane and dropping them by parachute!

4. ALEXANDER THE GREAT MAY HAVE BEEN ACCIDENTALLY BURIED ALIVE.

Some scientists think he suffered from Guillain-Barré syndrome, which would have left him paralyzed but aware of what was going on around him. Terrifying!

5. PRESIDENT LINCOLN HAD A BODYGUARD ON DUTY THE NIGHT HE WAS ASSASSINATED.

Unfortunately, the bodyguard left halfway through the play to drink at the bar next door.

6. VICE PRESIDENT KAMALA HARRIS'S STEPCHILDREN CALL HER "MOMALA." IT'S A PLAY ON HER NAME AND THE YIDDISH WORD FOR "LITTLE MOTHER."

7. THE ROMAN EMPEROR CALIGULA, KNOWN FOR HIS CRUELTY, ECCENTRICITY, AND POSSIBLE MADNESS, PLANNED TO MAKE HIS FAVORITE HORSE AN OFFICIAL CONSUL.

Ultimately, this did not happen, and some scholars think it was an attempt to insult the Roman Senate rather than an actual plan.

8. IN 2006, VICE PRESIDENT DICK CHENEY ACCIDENTALLY SHOT A FRIEND WHILE ON A HUNTING TRIP.

The friend survived...and later apologized to Cheney for the incident!

• 9 •

IN THE 1600S, KING
CHARLES XI OF SWEDEN
ATTEMPTED TO REPLACE
CAVALRY HORSES WITH A
NEW ANIMAL: THE MOOSE.

· 10 ·

GRIGORI RASPUTIN, RUSSIAN MYSTIC AND ADVISER TO TSAR NICHOLAS II, WAS NOTORIOUSLY HARD TO KILL; HE WAS POISONED, STABBED, SHOT, AND THROWN INTO FREEZING WATER BEFORE FINALLY SUCCUMBING TO HIS WOUNDS.

11. DURING HIS TIME AS LIBYA'S POLITICAL LEADER, MUAMMAR GADDAFI EMPLOYED AN ELITE GROUP OF ALL-FEMALE BODYGUARDS OFFICIALLY KNOWN AS THE REVOLUTIONARY NUNS.

They received special training in both martial arts and firearms, and were sworn to a life of celibacy.

12. PRESIDENTS JOHN ADAMS AND THOMAS JEFFERSON DIED WITHIN HOURS OF EACH OTHER.

Even stranger, the day they died was the Fourth of July.

13. THE FIRST WOMAN TO BE ELECTED MAYOR IN THE UNITED STATES WAS SUSANNA M. SALTER.

She had been added to the ballot by a group of men who hoped she would suffer a humiliating loss, discouraging female participation in politics. Instead, she won!

14. THERE WERE TECHNICALLY 14 PRESIDENTS BEFORE GEORGE WASHINGTON.

In the years between the signing of the Declaration of Independence and the ratification of the Constitution, 14 men held the title of "President of the United States in Congress Assembled"—effectively the country's top executive.

15. PING-PONG MATCHES PLAYED SUCH AN IMPORTANT ROLE IN THE NORMALIZATION OF US/CHINA RELATIONS THAT "PING-PONG DIPLOMACY" IS NOW AN ACCEPTED TERM.

16. THE OTTOMAN EMPIRE LASTED FROM THE YEAR 1299 ALL THE WAY UNTIL 1922.

In fact, the Ottomans were one of the combatants in WWI.

17. DECADES BEFORE THE INVENTION OF PHOTOSHOP, STALIN BECAME KNOWN FOR HAVING PHOTOGRAPHS "RETOUCHED" TO REMOVE UNDESIRABLES.

18. DURING HIS LIFE, CUBAN LEADER FIDEL CASTRO IS BELIEVED TO HAVE SURVIVED MORE THAN 600 ASSASSINATION ATTEMPTS.

19. PRESIDENT RONALD REAGAN AND HIS WIFE, NANCY, REGULARLY CONSULTED AN ASTROLOGER NAMED JOAN QUIGLEY.

She was said to have significant input on the president's schedule.

20. IN 1967, ACTIVIST ABBIE HOFFMAN STAGED AN EVENT WHERE HE PROMISED TO "LEVITATE THE PENTAGON" TO END THE VIETNAM WAR.

While this was obviously ridiculous, Hoffman had conceived the stunt as a way to highlight the absurdity of the war.

• 21 •

EGYPT'S KING FAROUK I
WAS A TOTAL KLEPTOMANIAC;
NOT ONLY DID HE HAVE A
HABIT OF PICKPOCKETING
COMMONERS FOR NO APPARENT
REASON, HE EVEN STOLE
THINGS FROM OTHER HEADS
OF STATE, INCLUDING WINSTON
CHURCHILL'S POCKET WATCH.

22. JEANNETTE RANKIN WAS THE FIRST WOMAN TO BE ELECTED TO CONGRESS.

She was elected in 1916...four years before the 19th Amendment granted women the right to vote.

23. AS HE LAY DYING, ENGLAND'S KING GEORGE V WAS EUTHANIZED BY HIS DOCTOR SO THE KING'S DEATH COULD BE ANNOUNCED IN THE MORNING PAPERS RATHER THAN THE EVENING ONES.

24. HATSHEPSUT WAS THE ONLY FEMALE PHARAOH IN RECORDED HISTORY.

She became the fifth pharaoh of the 18th Dynasty of ancient Egypt, after taking over as a supposed regent for her son, and reigned for over twenty years. While accounts seem to paint her reign as a favorable one, her images have been defaced on temples and inscriptions, as though the vandals meant to wipe her existence from history.

25. QUEEN LILI'UOKALANI WAS THE FIRST WOMAN EVER TO RULE THE KINGDOM OF HAWAII AND THE FIRST QUEEN REGNANT IN THE HISTORY OF HAWAII.

She was the last sovereign monarch until she was overthrown in a coup. She was also a gifted musician and singer and composed over 150 songs, including the ballad "Aloha 'Oe."

26. DURING A 1977 VISIT TO POLAND, PRESIDENT JIMMY CARTER'S TRANSLATOR WAS...NOT GOOD.

The interpreter caused much confusion by telling the Polish people that President Carter desired them "carnally" and was "happy to grasp at Poland's private parts."

27. HOLY ROMAN EMPEROR FREDERICK II WAS EXCOMMUNICATED BY THE CHURCH THREE DIFFERENT TIMES, AND POPE GREGORY IX EVEN SPECULATED THAT HE MIGHT BE A PRECURSOR TO THE ANTICHRIST.

28. CHINA'S ZHENGDE EMPEROR, WHO RULED FROM 1505 TO 1521, BUILT AN ENTIRE FAKE CITY MARKET INSIDE ONE OF HIS PALACES AND DEMANDED THAT HIS SERVANTS, GUARDS, AND OTHER ATTENDANTS PLAY THE ROLES OF MERCHANTS AND PASSERSBY SO HE COULD EXPERIENCE LIFE AS A COMMONER.

29. THE EMANCIPATION PROCLAMATION DIDN'T ACTUALLY END SLAVERY IN THE UNITED STATES; IT SPECIFICALLY ENDED SLAVERY ONLY IN THE STATES THAT WERE ACTIVELY REBELLING.

It wasn't until the 13th Amendment that slavery officially ended in America.

· 30 ·

SOME HISTORIANS BELIEVE
PRESIDENT ZACHARY
TAYLOR DIED WHEN HE
SUFFERED A LETHAL BOUT
OF GASTROENTERITIS AFTER
GORGING ON CHERRIES AND
MILK DURING A FOURTH OF
JULY CELEBRATION.

· 31 ·

POPULAR UNION ORGANIZER EUGENE V. DEBS RAN FOR PRESIDENT IN 1920 UNDER THE SOCIALIST PARTY TICKET—DESPITE BEING IN PRISON AT THE TIME.

His campaign buttons read, "Convict No. 9653 for President," and he received nearly 1 million votes.

32. IN ADDITION TO THE 13 ORIGINAL US STATES, THERE WAS ALMOST A 14TH STATE CALLED "FRANKLIN," MADE UP OF COUNTIES IN WHAT IS NOW TENNESSEE.

33. AN AMERICAN WARSHIP NAMED THE USS *WILLIAM D. PORTER* (NICKNAMED THE "WILLIE DEE") WAS KNOWN FOR A SERIES OF MISHAPS COMMITTED BY ITS CREW.

Most famously, the ship was part of a convoy in 1943 and accidentally launched a torpedo at the vessel carrying President Franklin D. Roosevelt during a training drill. Fortunately, they were able to alert FDR's ship in time to avoid disaster.

34. WHEN PRESIDENT WOODROW WILSON HAD A STROKE IN 1919, HIS WIFE, EDITH BOLLING GALT WILSON, EFFECTIVELY RAN THE COUNTRY UNTIL THE END OF HIS TERM.

She is sometimes colloquially called America's first female president.

35. EDWARD GIBBON WAKEFIELD IS CONSIDERED THE "FOUNDER" OF NEW ZEALAND, BUT BEFORE THAT HE WAS MOSTLY KNOWN AS A GUY WHO WENT TO JAIL FOR ABDUCTING AND MARRYING A 15-YEAR-OLD HEIRESS.

36. DUTCH PRIME MINISTER JOHAN DE WITT SUFFERED AN INTERESTING FATE: THE UNPOPULAR RULER WAS LYNCHED AND EATEN (YES, EATEN) BY HIS OWN CONSTITUENTS IN 1672.

37. DRACO THE LAWGIVER, A GREEK LEGISLATOR IN THE SEVENTH CENTURY BC, WAS RESPONSIBLE FOR CREATING A CODE OF LAWS IN ATHENS (SEE: "DRACONIAN LAW").

His death is a fascinating one: legend states that a crowd showered him with hats, shirts, and other clothing as a show of approval...but their approval was so aggressive that he suffocated beneath the pile.

38. IN 1836, AN ENTHUSIASTIC SUPPORTER GIFTED PRESIDENT ANDREW JACKSON A 1,400-LB. WHEEL OF CHEESE, WHICH STANK UP THE WHITE HOUSE FOR OVER A YEAR BEFORE JACKSON BEGGED AMERICAN CITIZENS TO COME TO THE WHITE HOUSE TO DEVOUR IT.

39. IN 1952, ALBERT EINSTEIN WAS OFFERED THE PRESIDENCY OF ISRAEL, BUT TURNED IT DOWN.

40. FRANCE'S CHARLES VI (ALSO KNOWN AS "CHARLES THE MAD") SUFFERED FROM SEVERE MENTAL ILLNESS.

One of its manifestations was a persistent belief that he was made of glass and might shatter if touched.

41. DURING THE COVID-19 PANDEMIC, CHINESE OFFICIALS BRIEFLY CAUSED A DIPLOMATIC INCIDENT WHEN THEY CONDUCTED "ANAL SWABBING" COVID TESTS ON AMERICAN OFFICIALS.

· 42 ·

PRESIDENT BILL CLINTON ONCE MISPLACED THE UNITED STATES' NUCLEAR LAUNCH CODES... FOR MONTHS.

· 43 ·

PRESIDENT ANDREW JACKSON TAUGHT HIS PARROT TO SWEAR SO SUCCESSFULLY AND COLORFULLY THAT IT HAD TO BE REMOVED FROM HIS FUNERAL DUE TO ITS FOUL (FOWL?) LANGUAGE.

44. CLEOPATRA MARRIED HER BROTHERS.

Yes, brothers—she had two and married them both.

45. NANCY PELOSI MAKES SURE THAT HER OFFICE IS STOCKED WITH GHIRARDELLI CHOCOLATES.

46. SOME SCHOLARS BELIEVE THE ROMAN EMPIRE HAD A TRANSGENDER RULER: EMPEROR ELAGABALUS PREFERRED TO BE CALLED A LADY RATHER THAN A LORD, WAS KNOWN TO WEAR WIGS AND MAKEUP, AND EVEN TRIED TO FIND A DOCTOR WHO COULD PERFORM A SEX REASSIGNMENT.

47. OSKALOOSA, KANSAS, BECAME THE FIRST TOWN IN THE UNITED STATES KNOWN TO HAVE AN ALL-WOMAN GOVERNMENT, WITH THE MAYOR AND ENTIRE COUNCIL BEING FEMALE.

The council included Mayor Mary D. Lowman and Council members Carrie Johnson, Sadie E. Balsley, Hanna P. Morse, Emma K. Hamilton, and Mittie Josephine Golden. One year prior to their election, in 1887, voters in Syracuse, Kansas, elected women to all five seats of the city council, but a man served as mayor.

48. THE BRITISH SUFFRAGETTES LEARNED JUJITSU TO DEFEND THEMSELVES AND EVADE ARREST.

Edith Margaret Garrud used her martial arts background to secretly train a unit of 30 members of the Women's Social and Political Union in self-defense. The group was alternately known as "the Bodyguard" and "the Amazons," and was highly effective at resisting arrest.

49. ROBERT SMALLS ESCAPED SLAVERY IN SOUTH CAROLINA BY STEALING A CONFEDERATE SHIP AND SAILING NORTH WITH IT.

He later returned to South Carolina, where he bought his former master's house and was later elected to Congress.

50. PRESIDENT JOHN QUINCY ADAMS HAD AN UNUSUAL MORNING ROUTINE: HE WOULD TRAVEL TO THE POTOMAC RIVER, REMOVE ALL OF HIS CLOTHES, AND GO SKINNY-DIPPING.

51. IN 1912, A WOULD-BE ASSASSIN SHOT TEDDY ROOSEVELT IN THE MIDDLE OF A CAMPAIGN SPEECH.

Fortunately for the former president, the bullet was slowed by the papers in his pocket, and he went right on giving his speech as if nothing had happened.

52. LONG BEFORE HE BECAME A BITTER ENEMY OF THE UNITED STATES, SADDAM HUSSEIN WAS AWARDED THE KEY TO THE CITY OF DETROIT, IN RECOGNITION OF SEVERAL CHARITABLE DONATIONS HE MADE IN THE AREA.

· 53 ·

IN 1920, MAHARAJA JAI SINGH, RULER OF THE INDIAN STATE OF ALWAR, ENTERED A ROLLS-ROYCE DEALERSHIP IN ENGLAND AND WAS TREATED POORLY BY THE SALESMEN.

Out of spite, he bought seven of the cars, shipped them back to India, and used them for garbage collection.

· 54 ·

WINSTON CHURCHILL ENJOYED SPENDING TIME NAKED.

President Franklin D. Roosevelt once accidentally walked in on Churchill relaxing in the nude during a visit to the White House.

55. IN 2005, PRESIDENT GEORGE W. BUSH WAS ALMOST KILLED BY A HAND GRENADE.

A Georgian protester managed to throw a grenade dangerously close to the president, but it simply failed to go off.

56. KING CHRISTIAN VII OF DENMARK HAD A... "SELF-PLEASURE" PROBLEM.

How big of a problem? Well, it's the main thing he's remembered for, so...pretty big.

57. IN 1698, RUSSIA'S TSAR PETER I ATTEMPTED TO FORCE RUSSIA TO BE MORE LIKE EUROPE IN THE STRANGEST WAY POSSIBLE: HE IMPOSED A BEARD TAX TO DISCOURAGE THE GROWING OF BEARDS.

58. IN 1994, RUSSIAN PRESIDENT BORIS YELTSIN WAS FOUND OUTSIDE THE WHITE HOUSE IN THE MIDDLE OF THE NIGHT WEARING ONLY HIS UNDERWEAR.

The reason? The very drunk president wanted to hail a cab so he could get a pizza.

59. STALIN KNEW ABOUT THE MANHATTAN PROJECT BEFORE PRESIDENT HARRY TRUMAN DID.

Truman only learned of its existence after FDR's death, while Stalin had a network of spies keeping him informed.

60. ELEANOR ROOSEVELT ONCE FLEW WITH AMELIA EARHART.

The aviator inspired Eleanor to apply for her own pilot's license and even took her on a flight from DC to Baltimore in 1933.

61. IN THE 1927 LIBERIAN GENERAL ELECTION, PRESIDENT CHARLES D. B. KING RECEIVED 240,000 VOTES...DESPITE THE FACT THAT THERE WERE JUST 15,000 REGISTERED VOTERS IN THE ENTIRE COUNTRY.

62. IN 2019, VOLODYMYR ZELENSKYY WAS ELECTED PRESIDENT OF UKRAINE.

Prior to his election, he was mostly known for his role in a political satire television show, where he played...the president of Ukraine.

63. FRENCH PRESIDENT FÉLIX FAURE DIED IN OFFICE.

Literally, in this case: he died from apoplexy while engaged in sexual activities with his mistress on top of the presidential desk.

64. POMPEY THE GREAT MARRIED JULIUS CAESAR'S DAUGHTER.

Some scholars believe he had divorced his previous wife for having an affair...with Julius Caesar.

· 65 ·

PEPI II, WHO RULED EGYPT
AROUND 2278 BC, DEMANDED
THAT HIS SLAVES COAT
THEMSELVES IN HONEY
SO THAT FLIES WOULD
BE ATTRACTED TO THEM
RATHER THAN HIM.

• 66 •

TSAR PETER III WAS OBSESSED WITH TOY SOLDIERS. IN FACT, ON THE NIGHT OF HIS WEDDING TO CATHERINE THE GREAT, HE ELECTED TO PLAY WITH HIS TOYS RATHER THAN CONSUMMATE THE MARRIAGE.

67. **MANY HISTORIANS BELIEVE THAT PRESIDENT JAMES BUCHANAN WAS GAY.**

William Rufus King, then a senator from Alabama, is believed to have been his lover.

68. **IN 1958, THE KGB ATTEMPTED TO BLACKMAIL INDONESIAN PRESIDENT SUKARNO WITH A FAKE SEX TAPE.**

Not only did their plan not work, Sukarno was apparently so thrilled that he asked the KGB for copies.

69. **RUTH BADER GINSBURG'S COLLARS WERE CODED.**

She would wear a lace collar featuring gold trim and charms when she had a majority opinion, and a mirrored bib necklace when her side had come up short.

70. **A RUSSIAN CON MAN NAMED BORIS SKOSSYREFF MANAGED TO HAVE HIMSELF CROWNED KING OF ANDORRA IN 1934, AND STAYED IN POWER FOR NEARLY TWO WEEKS BEFORE BEING ARRESTED BY SPANISH AUTHORITIES.**

71. **FROM 1513 TO 1972, DENMARK WAS RULED BY AN UNBROKEN STREAK OF MONARCHS NAMED EITHER CHRISTIAN OR FREDERICK.**

Christians II through X and Fredericks I through IX reigned for alternating periods during this time.

72. PRESIDENT LYNDON B. JOHNSON WAS FAMOUSLY PROUD OF HIS PENIS, WHICH HE NICKNAMED "JUMBO."

He was known for, uh, regularly displaying it to White House staffers.

73. JOHN HINCKLEY JR. HAD A VERY SPECIFIC REASON FOR TRYING TO ASSASSINATE PRESIDENT RONALD REAGAN: HE THOUGHT IT WOULD IMPRESS ACTRESS JODIE FOSTER.

74. PRESIDENT GERALD FORD IS THE ONLY PRESIDENT IN AMERICAN HISTORY WHO WAS NOT ELECTED TO EITHER THE PRESIDENCY OR VICE PRESIDENCY.

He was appointed as vice president following Spiro Agnew's resignation and became president after Richard Nixon's resignation.

75. WHEN NAPOLEON RETURNED FROM EXILE, AN ENTIRE INFANTRY REGIMENT WAS SENT TO STOP HIM.

Instead, Napoleon gained their loyalty, and they joined his ranks.

76. THE INITIAL "S" IN ULYSSES S. GRANT DOES NOT STAND FOR ANYTHING.

Interestingly, the "S" in Harry S. Truman also does not stand for anything.

• 77 •

TEDDY ROOSEVELT'S
DAUGHTER ALICE WAS
BARRED FROM THE WHITE
HOUSE WHEN IT WAS
DISCOVERED THAT SHE HAD
BURIED A VOODOO DOLL OF
THE INCOMING PRESIDENT'S
WIFE ON THE GROUNDS.

· 78 ·

BEFORE HIS TIME AS PRESIDENT, ABRAHAM LINCOLN WAS CHALLENGED TO A DUEL BY THE ILLINOIS STATE AUDITOR.

Lincoln demanded the duel be fought in a small pit on a remote island using only broadswords, and his intimidated opponent withdrew.

79. IN 1934, A GROUP OF WEALTHY BANKERS AND BUSINESSMEN ENGAGED IN A CONSPIRACY KNOWN AS THE "BUSINESS PLOT" TO OVERTHROW PRESIDENT FRANKLIN D. ROOSEVELT AND INSTALL RETIRED GENERAL SMEDLEY BUTLER AS THE FASCIST DICTATOR OF THE UNITED STATES. BUTLER WAS UNINTERESTED AND IMMEDIATELY REPORTED THE CONSPIRATORS FOR TREASON.

80. TRUE OR FALSE: J. EDGAR HOOVER WAS KNOWN TO ENJOY DRESSING IN WOMEN'S CLOTHING.

False. This persistent rumor is untrue, but it was gleefully spread by the many, many people whom Hoover wronged during his career.

81. TRUE OR FALSE: RUSSIA'S FEBRUARY REVOLUTION ACTUALLY TOOK PLACE IN MARCH, AND THE OCTOBER REVOLUTION ACTUALLY TOOK PLACE IN NOVEMBER.

True. The Russians were using the outdated Julian calendar system.

82. TRUE OR FALSE: HITLER WAS DEMOCRATICALLY ELECTED.

False. This popular myth is flat-out wrong. In fact, the Nazis never received more than 37% of the electoral vote. Hitler came to power when he was appointed chancellor by German president Hindenburg, and by the next "election" had made all other political parties illegal.

83. TRUE OR FALSE: ABRAHAM LINCOLN IS THE ONLY US PRESIDENT TO OWN A PATENT.

True. Lincoln patented a method of lifting boats over river obstructions in 1849.

84. TRUE OR FALSE: PRESIDENT JOHN QUINCY ADAMS HAD A PET ALLIGATOR, WHICH HE KEPT IN A WHITE HOUSE BATHTUB AND USED TO SCARE GUESTS.

False. Another persistent presidential rumor, this one does not appear to have any basis in fact. It's possible that President Adams was given an alligator at one point, but there's no evidence that he kept it as a pet.

85. TRUE OR FALSE: THE DECLARATION OF INDEPENDENCE WAS ACTUALLY SIGNED ON JULY 2, NOT JULY 4.

True. Some argue Independence Day should be celebrated on July 2. Ultimately, July 4 was selected because that's when the Declaration of Independence was approved by Congress.

86. TRUE OR FALSE: THE US GOVERNMENT HAS ONLY PAID OFF THE ENTIRE NATIONAL DEBT ONCE IN ITS ENTIRE HISTORY.

True. Andrew Jackson zeroed out the national debt in 1835 for the only time in American history. Unfortunately, the steps he took to achieve this probably contributed to a massive recession just two years later.

87. TRUE OR FALSE: FUTURE US ATTORNEY GENERAL JOHN ASHCROFT ONCE LOST AN ELECTION TO A DEAD MAN.

True. In 2000, Ashcroft lost a senate race to Missouri governor Mel Carnahan...who had been dead for more than a month.

· 88 ·

TRUE OR FALSE: PRESIDENT WILLIAM HOWARD TAFT WAS SO LARGE THAT HE ONCE BECAME STUCK IN THE WHITE HOUSE BATHTUB.

False. This is a popular "fun fact," but it has no basis in truth. That said, Taft did have an enormous, custom-made bathtub installed in the White House during his stay.

· 89 ·

TRUE OR FALSE: DONALD TRUMP WAS THE FIRST US PRESIDENT TO BE ARRESTED.

False. That honor goes to Ulysses S. Grant, who was arrested in 1872 for speeding recklessly down the streets of Washington, DC in a horse-drawn carriage.

90. TRUE OR FALSE: ABRAHAM LINCOLN'S SON, ROBERT TODD LINCOLN, WAS PRESENT AT THREE DIFFERENT PRESIDENTIAL ASSASSINATIONS.

False. While he does have loose connections to the assassinations, rumors of him being "present" are exaggerated. He did not attend the play where his father was killed, and while he was in Buffalo at the time McKinley was shot, he was nowhere near the president. He was, however, in the room when President Garfield was shot.

91. TRUE OR FALSE: HELEN KELLER WAS AN ACTIVE FIGURE IN SOCIALIST POLITICS.

True. She joined the Socialist Party in 1909 and was later a founding member of the American Civil Liberties Union.

92. TRUE OR FALSE: WOODROW WILSON IS THE ONLY US PRESIDENT TO HOLD A PHD.

True. Wilson obtained his doctorate in political science from Johns Hopkins University in 1886. He is the only president to have a doctorate.

93. TRUE OR FALSE: ROBERT F. KENNEDY WAS THE FIRST US PRESIDENTIAL CANDIDATE TO BE ASSASSINATED.

False. Interestingly enough, that honor belongs to Joseph Smith, founder of the Latter-Day Saint movement and 1844 presidential candidate.

94. **TRUE OR FALSE: A STATE ONCE TRIED TO PASS A BILL THAT WOULD LEGALLY DECLARE THE VALUE OF PI TO BE 3.2.**

True. Amazingly enough, Indiana did just that in 1897. The bill passed the state House of Representatives, but was promptly killed in the Senate.

95. **TRUE OR FALSE: ONE OF THE REASONS CLEOPATRA IS REMARKABLE IS THAT SHE WAS THE EARLIEST RECORDED FEMALE HEAD OF STATE.**

False. Women have held positions of power for millennia. For example, Sumeria is one of the oldest known civilizations, and its powerful city-state of Kish had a female ruler as early as 2500 BC.

96. **TRUE OR FALSE: ENGLAND ONCE HAD A KING WHO COULD NOT SPEAK ENGLISH.**

True. England's King Richard I—also known as Richard the Lionheart—couldn't speak a word of English.

97. **TRUE OR FALSE: ONE OF MARGARET THATCHER'S NICKNAMES WAS "THATCHER THE MILK SNATCHER."**

True. She was given the nickname after she sponsored legislation to eliminate the free milk program for students over the age of seven in order to cut costs for schools.

98. **TRUE OR FALSE: A SITTING US PRESIDENT HAS NEVER LED TROOPS INTO BATTLE.**

False. It has happened exactly once: George Washington personally took charge of his troops while putting down the Whiskey Rebellion.

TRUE OR FALSE: THE US SENATE HAS A DESIGNATED "CANDY DESK."

True. Every term, one desk is designated the "candy desk," and its occupant is responsible for keeping it stocked with candy for the next two years. The tradition started in 1965.

TRUE OR FALSE: PRESIDENT LYNDON B. JOHNSON DROVE AN AMPHIBIOUS CAR.

True. Johnson owned one of the few "Amphicars," which were capable of driving on both land and water. He liked to play pranks on his passengers by driving straight into the water.

War

Ernest Hemingway once wrote, "Never think that war, no matter how necessary, nor how justified, is not a crime." But while finding humor in war is not easy, the history of warfare presents no end of interesting and fascinating stories. From the dog who was awarded two Blue Cross medals to the inflatable balloon tanks used to confuse the Nazis, war has produced a seemingly endless number of head-scratching and perplexing tales. Frankly, you haven't lived until you've heard about the time Adolf Hitler tried to kidnap the pope.

1. IN 1925, A WAR BETWEEN GREECE AND BULGARIA STARTED WHEN A GREEK SOLDIER WAS SHOT AFTER CROSSING THE BULGARIAN BORDER TO CHASE AFTER HIS DOG. THE WAR, APPROPRIATELY, IS NOW KNOWN AS THE WAR OF THE STRAY DOG.

2. IN 2011, THE US GOVERNMENT DRAFTED CONPLAN 8888-11: AN OFFICIAL DEPARTMENT OF DEFENSE DOCUMENT DETAILING A PLAN TO DEAL WITH A ZOMBIE APOCALYPSE.

In fairness to the government, the plan was somewhat tongue-in-cheek, designed to help develop relevant skills and strategies in a deliberately ridiculous situation.

3. JAPANESE INTELLIGENCE OFFICER HIROO ONODA WAS STATIONED ON AN ISLAND IN THE PHILIPPINES DURING WWII, AND NEVER RECEIVED WORD THAT THE WAR HAD ENDED.

He remained there for 29 years, until his former commanding officer personally arrived to relieve him of duty.

4. THE "WAR OF JENKINS'S EAR" BROKE OUT IN 1739, AFTER A BRITISH TRADER NAMED ROBERT JENKINS HAD HIS EAR CUT OFF BY SPANISH SAILORS UPON BEING ACCUSED OF SMUGGLING.

Some estimates place the death toll of this war over an ear between 35,000 and 50,000.

5. SOVIET CASUALTIES DURING WWII WERE SO GREAT THAT 68% OF RUSSIAN MALES BORN IN 1923 DID NOT LIVE TO SEE THE END OF THE WAR.

6. IN 1945, THE MAKER OF CROSSWORD PUZZLES FOR BRITAIN'S *THE DAILY TELEGRAPH* WAS BRIEFLY SUSPECTED OF BEING A GERMAN SPY, WHEN D-DAY RELATED CODEWORDS KEPT RANDOMLY APPEARING IN HIS CROSSWORDS IN THE DAYS LEADING UP TO THE ASSAULT.

7. THE FIRST BATTLE OF BULL RUN IN THE AMERICAN CIVIL WAR WAS KNOWN AS THE "PICNIC BATTLE" BECAUSE SO MANY CIVILIANS SET UP PICNICS ON THE FRINGES OF THE FIGHT TO WATCH THE BATTLE TAKE PLACE.

8. IN 1597, LEGENDARY KOREAN ADMIRAL YI SUN-SIN DEFEATED THE JAPANESE IN A NAVAL ENGAGEMENT DURING WHICH HE WAS OUTNUMBERED 333 SHIPS TO 13.

9. IN 1943, HITLER (ALLEGEDLY) ORDERED THE SS TO KIDNAP THE POPE.

· 10 ·

IN THE 1930S, AUSTRALIA DECLARED WAR ON THE COUNTRY'S EMU POPULATION...AND LOST.

The "Emu War," as it came to be known, resulted in the deaths of less than 1,000 emus, and the birds remain extremely common in Australia today.

• 11 •

IN 1958, THE US AIR FORCE DEVELOPED PROJECT A119: A TOP-SECRET PLAN WITH THE AIM OF DETONATING A NUCLEAR BOMB ON THE MOON.

Because the explosion would be visible from Earth, it was believed that this show of force would raise American spirits and spook the Soviet Union.

12. THE AMERICAN CIVIL WAR INCLUDED CONFLICTS AS FAR AWAY AS BRAZIL; IN 1864, THE USS *WACHUSETT* CAPTURED THE CSS *FLORIDA* IN BRAZIL'S PORT OF SALVADOR, SCORING A VICTORY FOR UNION FORCES.

Brazil, predictably, was not thrilled with this violation of its sovereignty.

13. THE BATTLE OF TANGA WAS A WWI BATTLE THAT TOOK PLACE IN GERMAN EAST AFRICA.

Despite outnumbering the German forces by roughly 9–1, the British were defeated...in part because a large portion of their forces was swarmed by angry bees. The battle is colloquially known as the "Battle of the Bees."

14. KING JOHN OF BOHEMIA DIED FIGHTING IN THE BATTLE OF CRÉCY IN 1346.

Impressive though it is that a king would lead his troops into battle, King John had one small problem: he had been blind for more than a decade.

15. THE VIKING WARRIOR SIGURD THE MIGHTY WAS KILLED BY A SEVERED HEAD: AFTER TAKING THE HEAD OF HIS ENEMY, MÁEL BRIGTE, ONE OF THE DECEASED'S TEETH PIERCED HIS LEG.

The wound soon became infected, and eventually claimed Sigurd's life.

16. DURING WWII, A GERMAN U-BOAT WAS DESTROYED BECAUSE OF A TOILET ACCIDENT.

One of the submarine's high-pressure toilets malfunctioned, forcing the sub to surface, where it was discovered and destroyed by British forces.

17. THE SHORTEST WAR IN HISTORY IS BELIEVED TO BE THE ANGLO-ZANZIBAR WAR, WHICH LASTED A GRAND TOTAL OF LESS THAN 45 MINUTES.

18. THE SOVIETS PARTIED SO HARD AFTER THE END OF WWII THAT RUSSIA COMPLETELY RAN OUT OF VODKA FOR A TIME.

19. THE NAZI WAR MACHINE WAS FUELED BY TRULY UNBELIEVABLE AMOUNTS OF METH.

Pervitin, an early methamphetamine, was commonly available in Nazi Germany and distributed to German soldiers in massive quantities.

20. THE ONLY WWII CASUALTIES ON US SOIL CAME WHEN A BALLOON BOMB LAUNCHED FROM JAPAN DETONATED ON AN OREGON WOMAN AND SEVERAL CHILDREN IN 1945.

· 21 ·

A GREAT DANE NAMED JULIANA RECEIVED A BLUE CROSS MEDAL DURING WWII AFTER SHE EXTINGUISHED AN INCENDIARY BOMB BY URINATING ON IT.

It was the first of two Blue Cross medals she would be awarded during the war!

· 22 ·

IN 2010, THE NICARAGUAN ARMY ACCIDENTALLY "INVADED" COSTA RICA WHEN GOOGLE MAPS ALLEGEDLY LED THEM OVER THE BORDER BY MISTAKE.

23. IT SOUNDS LIKE SOMETHING OUT OF *BLAZING SADDLES*, BUT IT'S TRUE: DURING WWI, THE FRENCH CREATED AN ENTIRELY FAKE PARIS OUT OF WOOD AND CANVAS TO CONFUSE GERMAN BOMBERS FLYING AT NIGHT.

24. TSUTOMU YAMAGUCHI WAS PRESENT AT BOTH THE BOMBING OF HIROSHIMA AND THE BOMBING OF NAGASAKI.

Somehow, he managed to survive both blasts.

25. IN THE HISTORY OF WARFARE, A SUBMERGED SUBMARINE HAS ONLY SUNK ANOTHER SUBMERGED SUBMARINE ONE TIME.

The British HMS *Venturer* sank the German *U-864* in 1945, as WWII neared its end.

26. IN 1986, AMERICAN BOMBERS DROPPED A SERIES OF EXPLOSIVES ON AN UNDERSEA VOLCANO AFTER MISTAKENLY IDENTIFYING THE STEAM RISING FROM THE WATER AS EVIDENCE OF A LIBYAN SUBMARINE.

Also worth noting: Libya had no submarines at this time.

27. WHEN THE JAPANESE NAVY LAUNCHED THE MASSIVE BATTLESHIP *MUSASHI* IN 1940, IT DISPLACED SO MUCH WATER THAT IT ACCIDENTALLY FLOODED THE COASTAL AREAS OF NAGASAKI.

28. IN 1967, ISRAEL WAS ATTACKED BY A COALITION OF EGYPT, SYRIA, JORDAN, IRAQ, AND SAUDI ARABIA.

Not only did Israel win this war, it did so in six days—capturing effectively the entire Sinai Peninsula in the process.

29. IN THE MID-1800S, AN AMERICAN NAMED WILLIAM WALKER DECLARED HIMSELF THE PRESIDENT OF NICARAGUA AFTER SEIZING CONTROL OF THE CAPITAL WITH A MERCENARY ARMY.

His reign was brief, brutal, and unpopular, and moves like relegalizing slavery and threatening his neighbors eventually led to his removal and execution. Ed Harris starred in a movie about his life, simply titled *Walker*.

30. AFTER WWI, THE FRENCH BUILT A SERIES OF FORTIFICATIONS CALLED THE MAGINOT LINE, DESIGNED TO PREVENT OR SLOW A FUTURE GERMAN INVASION.

During WWII, the Germans overcame this obstacle by...simply going around it.

31. 5,440 ALLIED SOLDIERS DIED DURING LIVE-FIRE DRILLS TRAINING FOR THE D-DAY INVASION.

That means roughly 1,000 more soldiers died during training than during the D-Day landing itself.

• 32 •

DURING WWI, THE GERMANS DISGUISED ONE OF THEIR CRUISERS AS A BRITISH OCEAN LINER.

Unfortunately for them, the ruse was discovered when the cruiser accidentally encountered the RMS *Carmania*... otherwise known as the exact ship it was disguised as.

· 33 ·

**DURING WWII, THE
AMERICANS USED
INFLATABLE TANKS TO
FOOL THE NAZIS.**

34. HERMANN GÖRING WAS A HIGH-RANKING NAZI OFFICER EVENTUALLY NAMED AS HITLER'S SUCCESSOR.

His brother Albert walked a different path, effectively using his brother's name and influence to save as many Jews as he could from the Holocaust.

35. THE US MILITARY IS MISSING AT LEAST SIX OF ITS NUCLEAR WEAPONS.

36. JUAN PUJOL GARCÍA WAS A DOUBLE AGENT WHO WORKED FOR THE BRITISH DURING WWII.

He was so good at his job that he wound up receiving major awards from both sides of the conflict: he was awarded the Iron Cross by the Nazis and made a Member of the Order of the British Empire by the British.

37. IN 1777, 16-YEAR-OLD SYBIL LUDINGTON RODE MORE THAN TWICE AS FAR AS PAUL REVERE TO WARN MILITIAMEN THAT THE BRITISH WERE COMING.

She is said to have made an all-night ride 40 miles to rally militia forces after Danbury, Connecticut, had been set ablaze by British forces.

38. THE LAST REMAINING RECIPIENT OF A CIVIL WAR PENSION DIED IN 2020.

Irene Triplett had been collecting her father's pension since his death in 1938. She was also the last remaining child of a Civil War veteran.

39. A BRITISH OFFICER NAMED DIGBY TATHAM-WARTER ONCE CAPTURED A GERMAN ARMORED CAR DURING WWII BY STICKING AN UMBRELLA THROUGH THE OBSERVATIONAL SLIT AND POKING THE DRIVER IN THE EYE.

He was famous for carrying the umbrella throughout the war.

40. CLARA BARTON, FOUNDER OF THE AMERICAN RED CROSS, WAS A NURSE DURING THE CIVIL WAR AND SET UP THE "OFFICE OF MISSING SOLDIERS" IN DOWNTOWN DC AFTER THE WAR.

Out of 63,000 inquiries, she ended up locating over 22,000 missing soldiers and arranged proper burials for 13,000 soldiers who died in the Confederate Andersonville Prison camp.

41. JOSEPHINE BAKER SMUGGLED MESSAGES TO FRENCH SOLDIERS DURING WWII.

A well-known singer and performer, she carefully concealed the hidden messages in clever ways, often using invisible ink to hide them in her sheet music or simply tucking them inside her dress.

· 42 ·

MEXICAN GENERAL SANTA ANNA HAD HIS LEG AMPUTATED AFTER BEING HIT BY CANNON FIRE IN 1838.

Four years later, he ordered it exhumed and gave it a full state burial.

· 43 ·

IN 1941, A SOVIET NAVAL CAPTAIN GAVE A BRITISH SUBMARINE CAPTAIN AN UNUSUAL GIFT: A LIVE REINDEER.

The British loaded it onto the submarine through a torpedo tube and eventually donated it to a British zoo.

44. THE ASSASSINATION OF ARCHDUKE FRANZ FERDINAND—WHICH KICKED OFF WWI—ONLY HAPPENED BECAUSE OF AN INCREDIBLE COINCIDENCE.

After a botched first attempt on the archduke's life, assassin Gavrilo Princip found himself nearly face-to-face with Ferdinand when his driver made a wrong turn and stalled the engine attempting to reverse.

45. DURING WWII, THE BRITISH ONCE DRESSED A DEAD BODY IN A ROYAL MARINES UNIFORM AND PUT FAKE WAR PLANS IN THE POCKET TO MISLEAD THE GERMANS.

And it worked!

46. CHINA'S BLOODY TAIPING REBELLION IN THE MID-1800S WAS LED BY HONG XIUQUAN, A RELIGIOUS LEADER WHO CLAIMED TO BE THE BROTHER OF JESUS CHRIST.

47. HARRIET TUBMAN CARRIED A REVOLVER AND WAS NOT AFRAID TO USE IT; SHE LATER RECALLED POINTING IT AT A FUGITIVE SLAVE'S HEAD WHEN MORALE WAS LOW AND SAYING, "YOU GO ON OR YOU DIE."

48. JOAN OF ARC SAID THAT AT THE AGE OF 13, SHE STARTED SEEING VISIONS OF ANGELS.

She continued to see these visions the rest of her life and claimed that they would guide her in how to support French King Charles VII against the English.

49. DURING WWII, THE SOVIETS TRAINED "ANTI-TANK DOGS" TO PLANT BOMBS ON GERMAN TANKS.

However, because they had been trained on Soviet tanks, they had an unfortunate habit of targeting those tanks instead.

50. SHORTLY AFTER HITLER'S DEATH, ONE OF THE STRANGEST BATTLES OF WWII OCCURRED: DURING THE BATTLE OF CASTLE ITTER, ALLIED AND GERMAN SOLDIERS FOUGHT ON THE SAME SIDE AGAINST WAFFEN-SS TROOPS.

51. "MAD JACK" CHURCHILL WAS THE LAST KNOWN MAN TO KILL AN ENEMY WITH A LONGBOW...IN 1941!

Unsurprisingly, the British soldier was the only man to record a kill with a longbow during WWII.

• 52 •

IN 1782, A WOMAN NAMED DEBORAH SAMPSON DISGUISED HERSELF AS A MAN TO FIGHT IN THE AMERICAN REVOLUTION.

She was so determined to evade discovery that she once dug a bullet out of her own leg to avoid risking a doctor finding out her secret.

• 53 •

DURING WWII, THE SOVIET AIR FORCE HAD AN ALL-FEMALE GROUP OF BOMBER PILOTS.

They were so successful that the Germans took to calling them "The Night Witches."

54. GERMANY ONLY CONDUCTED ONE MILITARY OPERATION ON NORTH AMERICAN SOIL DURING WWII: THE ERECTION OF AN AUTOMATED WEATHER STATION IN NORTHERN CANADA.

Their efforts to disguise the station were not very successful: one canister was mistakenly marked "Canadian Meteor Service" instead of the intended "Canadian Weather Service."

55. EDITH CAVELL WAS A BRITISH NURSE WHO WORKED IN GERMAN-OCCUPIED BELGIUM DURING WWI AND TREATED SOLDIERS REGARDLESS OF THEIR NATIONALITIES.

She also helped smuggle more than 200 British, French, and Belgian soldiers into Holland to escape the Germans.

56. ALTHOUGH NOOR INAYAT KHAN DID NOT HAVE A TALENT FOR ESPIONAGE, SHE BECAME A WIRELESS OPERATOR IN OCCUPIED FRANCE DURING WWII.

After almost all of her fellow agents were caught, she nearly single-handedly carried on managing spy radio traffic while on the run for four months, until she was betrayed and captured by the Nazis.

57. AUDIE MURPHY IS MOSTLY KNOWN FOR HIS INCREDIBLE FILM ACTING CAREER, BUT BEFORE THAT HE WAS THE MOST DECORATED SOLDIER IN AMERICAN HISTORY.

58. ANDREW JACKSON (WHO WOULD LATER BECOME PRESIDENT) DEFEATED THE BRITISH AT THE BATTLE OF NEW ORLEANS IN WHAT WOULD BE ONE OF THE ONLY AMERICAN VICTORIES IN THE WAR OF 1812.

The only problem? The peace treaty ending the war had been signed 15 days earlier.

59. THE LONGEST CONTINUOUS BATTLE IN HISTORY WAS THE BATTLE OF VERDUN DURING WWI.

That single engagement lasted an incredible 11 months, stretching from February to December 1916.

60. DOUGLAS BADER WAS AN RAF PILOT DURING WWII WITH AN UNUSUAL DISTINCTION: HE HAD NO LEGS.

He was eventually shot down and captured by the Germans, and attempted to escape his captors so many times that they threatened to take away his prosthetics.

61. DURING WWII, THE UNITED STATES EXPERIMENTED WITH "BAT BOMBS."

These bombs were designed to release thousands of bats, each with a small incendiary device attached to it, to start fires in enemy territory.

· 62 ·

IN 1950, THE US NAVY CONDUCTED A SECRET BIOLOGICAL WARFARE EXPERIMENT AGAINST ITS OWN PEOPLE BY SPRAYING "HARMLESS" BACTERIA OVER SAN FRANCISCO AND STUDYING DISPERSION PATTERNS TO GAUGE HOW VULNERABLE AMERICAN CITIES MIGHT BE TO SUCH ATTACKS.

Fig 1.

Fig 2.

· 63 ·

THE ANCIENT INVENTOR ARCHIMEDES IS CREDITED WITH THE CREATION OF MULTIPLE "SUPERWEAPONS" OF HIS TIME, INCLUDING A GIANT CLAW DESIGNED TO LIFT SHIPS OUT OF THE WATER AND A "HEAT RAY" THAT USED MIRRORS TO SET ENEMY SHIPS ON FIRE.

64. WHILE HARRIET TUBMAN WAS STILL ENSLAVED, AN OVERSEER THREW A TWO-LB. WEIGHT AT A FELLOW FIELD HAND AS THEY ATTEMPTED TO FLEE, BUT IT STRUCK HARRIET INSTEAD AND, IN HER WORDS, "BROKE MY SKULL."

She suffered lifelong headaches, seizures, and vivid dreams.

65. WWII BRITISH SPECIAL OPERATIONS EXECUTIVE AGENT PEARL WITHERINGTON'S MEMOIR SHARES MANY OF THE STRANGE BUT TRUE STORIES OF HER TIME AS AN SOE AGENT—EVERYTHING FROM DIVING INTO A CORNFIELD TO AVOID GERMAN FIRE, TO NEARLY BEING KILLED BY A RESISTANCE LEADER WHO DOUBTED HER IDENTITY, TO KEEPING A PET RABBIT THAT CAME WITH HER TO SO MANY DANGEROUS PLACES THAT IT BECAME OBLIVIOUS TO MACHINE-GUN FIRE.

66. DURING WWII, A SMALL BRITISH VESSEL RAMMED A MUCH LARGER GERMAN VESSEL IN A FINAL ACT OF DESPERATION.

The German captain was so impressed that he wrote to the British admiralty to recommend the British captain be recognized for his bravery.

67. CARROTS AREN'T ACTUALLY GOOD FOR YOUR EYES, BUT THE MYTH ORIGINATED AS BRITISH PROPAGANDA DURING WWII.

They wanted the Germans to believe the British had excellent eyesight.

68. THE FINAL CIVIL WAR CASUALTY OCCURRED IN 1914—ROUGHLY 50 YEARS AFTER THE WAR.

At the age of 85, Joshua Chamberlain finally succumbed to a lingering injury obtained during the war.

69. A SOLAR ECLIPSE ONCE ENDED A WAR.

In the 6th century BC, a battle between the Lydians and the Medes was interrupted by what historians believe was a solar eclipse. Both sides were so stunned that they stopped the battle and, subsequently, the entire war.

70. AFTER WWII, SUSAN TRAVERS (A BRITISH NURSE AND AMULANCE DRIVER WHO SERVED IN THE FRENCH RED CROSS DURING THE WAR) APPLIED TO BECOME AN OFFICIAL MEMBER OF THE FRENCH FOREIGN LEGION.

She did not specify her gender on the application, and it was accepted, essentially rubber-stamped by an officer who knew and admired her, making her the only woman to ever serve in the French Foreign Legion.

71. WHEN ROMAN EMPEROR VALERIAN WAS CAPTURED BY SHAPUR I, THE KING OF PERSIA, HE WAS FORCED TO ACT AS A HUMAN FOOTSTOOL WHENEVER SHAPUR WANTED TO MOUNT HIS HORSE.

72. FORMER PRUSSIAN MILITARY OFFICER BARON VON STEUBEN IMPLEMENTED THE TRAINING PROGRAM THAT HELPED THE CONTINENTAL ARMY WIN THE REVOLUTIONARY WAR.

He was also homosexual, and openly so—by the standards of the 18th century, anyway.

73. GEORGE WASHINGTON WAS POSTHUMOUSLY PROMOTED IN 1976 TO ENSURE THAT HE REMAINED THE HIGHEST RANKED MILITARY OFFICER IN AMERICAN HISTORY.

74. BETWEEN WWI AND WWII, THE US MILITARY DRAFTED PLANS FOR A THEORETICAL FUTURE WAR AGAINST GREAT BRITAIN THAT INCLUDED A DETAILED STRATEGY FOR THE INVASION OF CANADA.

75. AT THE BEGINNING OF WWII, BRITISH CITIZENS EUTHANIZED AN ESTIMATED 750,000 DOGS, CATS, AND OTHER PETS IN PREPARATION FOR ANTICIPATED FOOD SHORTAGES.

The event became known as the "British Pet Massacre."

76. GENGHIS KHAN KILLED SO MANY PEOPLE DURING HIS CONQUESTS THAT IT MEASURABLY LOWERED THE AMOUNT OF CARBON DIOXIDE IN THE ATMOSPHERE.

77. ARGUABLY THE LARGEST NAVAL BATTLE IN HISTORY HAPPENED IN 256 BC.

The Battle of Cape Ecnomus was fought between Rome and Carthage, and that lone battle resulted in roughly 50,000 total deaths.

78. IN THE 4TH CENTURY BC, THE THEBAN MILITARY FORMED AN ELITE UNIT KNOWN AS THE "SACRED BAND OF THEBES," WHICH WAS MADE UP OF 150 GAY MALE COUPLES.

It apparently paid off: the Sacred Band of Thebes is known for several significant victories over the legendary Spartans.

79. ON D-DAY, THE USS *TEXAS* BATTLESHIP INTENTIONALLY FLOODED PART OF ITS HULL IN ORDER TO TILT THE SHIP TO THE CORRECT ANGLE TO REACH GERMAN TARGETS FARTHER INLAND.

80. THE FIRST BATTLE OF THE AMERICAN CIVIL WAR WAS FOUGHT OUTSIDE WILMER MCLEAN'S HOUSE NEAR MANASSAS, VIRGINIA, AND THE TREATY THAT ENDED THE WAR WAS SIGNED IN HIS LIVING ROOM.

· 81 ·

TRUE OR FALSE: THE KING OF SIAM OFFERED A GROUP OF "WAR ELEPHANTS" TO ABRAHAM LINCOLN TO HELP HIM FIGHT THE CONFEDERACY.

False. This myth is commonly believed, partly because the King of Siam really did offer elephants to the United States. But it was President Buchanan he offered them to, and not as tools of war.

· 82 ·

TRUE OR FALSE: DURING THE REVOLUTIONARY WAR, A BRITISH SNIPER HAD A CLEAR SHOT AT GEORGE WASHINGTON BUT REFUSED TO SHOOT BECAUSE HE CONSIDERED IT WRONG TO SHOOT A MAN IN THE BACK.

True. Respected sniper Patrick Ferguson could have changed the course of history, but held his fire.

83. TRUE OR FALSE: SUBMARINES WERE USED DURING THE REVOLUTIONARY WAR.

True. Well, at least one was. Shocking though it may seem, the first submarine to be used in combat was the *Turtle*, with which the Americans attempted to sink British warships in 1775.

84. TRUE OR FALSE: THE BRITISH USED SEMEN AS INVISIBLE INK DURING WWI.

True. During WWI, a British captain named Mansfield Cumming discovered this...unique method of sending secret messages.

85. TRUE OR FALSE: THE UNITED STATES MILITARY ONCE HAD A "CAMEL CORPS."

True. In the mid-1800s, the United States experimented with camels as pack animals for the army. It didn't go great.

86. TRUE OR FALSE: HONDURAS AND EL SALVADOR ONCE WENT TO WAR OVER A SOCCER (FOOTBALL) MATCH.

False. A contentious match between the two nations may have served as the flashpoint for "The Football War," but tensions between the two nations had been building for some time. The game and the ensuing riot were simply the match that lit the flame.

87. TRUE OR FALSE: FOR ABOUT 20 YEARS DURING THE COLD WAR, THE US NUCLEAR LAUNCH CODES WERE "12345."

False. But the reality is just as dumb: they were actually 00000000.

88. TRUE OR FALSE: THE ROMANS ONCE LOST MORE SOLDIERS IN A SINGLE BATTLE THAN THE UNITED STATES LOST IN THE ENTIRE VIETNAM WAR.

True. Roman losses at the Battle of Cannae are estimated at 60,000–70,000. The United States lost just over 58,000 troops in Vietnam.

89. TRUE OR FALSE: NAGASAKI WAS INTENDED AS THE FIRST ATOMIC BOMB TARGET, BUT PLANES WERE DIVERTED TO HIROSHIMA DUE TO CLOUD COVER.

False. In fact, Nagasaki was never intended to be a target at all. The second bomb was meant for Kokura, but poor weather forced the bombers to go with their fallback option.

90. TRUE OR FALSE: AFTER WWII, THE SON OF AMERICAN GENERAL GEORGE S. PATTON BECAME CLOSE FRIENDS WITH THE SON OF GERMAN FIELD MARSHAL ERWIN ROMMEL.

True. In fact, the son of British general Bernard Montgomery became close with both as well.

91. TRUE OR FALSE: THE CITY OF NASHVILLE BANNED PROSTITUTION DURING THE CIVIL WAR.

False. In fact, they legalized it! So many Union soldiers were being struck down with sexually transmitted diseases that the city needed a way to regulate the practice.

92. TRUE OR FALSE: THERE WAS ONCE A WAR THAT LASTED 335 YEARS WITHOUT A SINGLE DROP OF BLOOD BEING SPILLED.

True. The Netherlands declared war on the Isles of Scilly in 1651 and just...forgot to ever make peace. The oversight was noticed and rectified 335 years later, in 1986.

93. TRUE OR FALSE: A NATIVE AMERICAN SOLDIER BECAME A WAR CHIEF DURING WWII.

True. Joseph Medicine Crow touched an enemy without killing him, took an enemy's weapon, stole an enemy's horse, and led a successful war party, all against the Nazis—making him the final member of the Crow tribe to become a war chief.

94. TRUE OR FALSE: DURING THE NAPOLEONIC WARS, AN ENGLISH TOWN PUT A MONKEY TO DEATH FOR BEING A FRENCH SPY.

True. Well...it's supposedly true, anyway! The monkey was the only survivor of a shipwreck and was dressed in a French Army uniform. Since the locals had never seen a monkey before, they... made some assumptions.

95. TRUE OR FALSE: THE LAST REMAINING UNDETONATED WWII BOMBS WERE LOCATED AND DISPOSED OF IN 2013.

False. In fact, historians estimate that there are probably thousands of tons of unexploded munitions left undiscovered in Germany alone.

96. TRUE OR FALSE: PEPSI BRIEFLY OWNED THE SIXTH-LARGEST NAVY IN THE WORLD.

True. In 1989, the Soviet Union signed a strange deal: they imported $3 billion worth of Pepsi in exchange for 17 obsolete submarines and 3 warships.

97. TRUE OR FALSE: DURING WWII, ONE MAN FOUGHT FOR THE JAPANESE, SOVIETS, AND GERMANS.

True. Yang Kyoungjong was a Korean conscripted into the Japanese army, captured and conscripted by the Soviets, then captured and conscripted by the Germans. American soldiers eventually captured him, but fortunately did not conscript him into the US Army.

98. TRUE OR FALSE: THE US MILITARY ONCE TRIED TO CREATE A "GAY BOMB."

True. It never got out of the proposal stage, but an Air Force lab wanted to create a biological weapon capable of inducing irresistible homosexual behavior in enemy soldiers. Huh.

99. TRUE OR FALSE: THE HEAD OF THE NAZI "SPECIAL PROJECTS DIVISION" WAS A MAN NICKNAMED "DEATHSHEAD" WHO WAS KNOWN FOR EXPERIMENTING WITH ROBOTIC AUGMENTATION AND CORPSE REANIMATION.

False. He's a great villain in the *Wolfenstein* video games, though.

· 100 ·

TRUE OR FALSE: HEMORRHOIDS PLAYED A ROLE IN NAPOLEON'S DOWNFALL.

True. At least, very likely true! Napoleon was known to suffer from hemorrhoids, and some historians believe that a particularly painful hemorrhoid prevented him from riding his horse during the Battle of Waterloo, contributing to his defeat.

Society
& Culture

Society is always evolving, and hindsight often begets regrets. Consider how we look back on shoulder pads and leg warmers—and then think about the fact that those trends are only a few decades old. It should come as little surprise, then, to discover that societies and cultures across the globe have more than a few regrettable habits and trends of their own. Or that even the greatest artists sometimes had a penchant for toilet humor (looking at you, Mozart).

1. GRAFFITI HASN'T CHANGED MUCH OVER THE YEARS.

In the ruins of Pompeii, you can find familiar messages like "Gaius was here" carved into walls.

2. UNTIL JUST AFTER WWII, MAY 1ST WAS KNOWN AS "MOVING DAY" IN NEW YORK CITY.

Why? Because at midnight, all leases in the city officially expired, leading to chaos as thousands upon thousands of people took to the streets to find new residences.

3. THE ROMANS USED HUMAN URINE AS MOUTHWASH.

They believed it helped clean and whiten their teeth. Yikes!

4. IN 1963, A TURKISH MAN REMOVED A WALL IN HIS BASEMENT AND ACCIDENTALLY DISCOVERED THE LOST UNDERGROUND CITY OF DERINKUYU, WHICH WAS ONCE HOME TO 20,000 PEOPLE.

5. NERO, THE FIFTH ROMAN EMPEROR, WAS MARRIED FIVE TIMES—AND HIS FINAL TWO MARRIAGES WERE TO MEN.

He first married Sporus, who was said to resemble one of his late wives, and later Pythagoras (no, not that one).

6. POPE GREGORY IX DECLARED WAR ON CATS: HE ISSUED A PROCLAMATION PRONOUNCING THAT CATS BORE SATAN'S SPIRIT.

Followers of the church responded by killing cats in such great numbers that the rat population boomed; this is believed to have contributed to the rise of the bubonic plague.

7. THE GLADIATORS OF ANCIENT ROME WEREN'T JUST MEN.

A female gladiator was known as a gladiatrix, and while they were relatively rare compared to male gladiators, they were celebrated as exotic spectacles.

8. THE OLYMPICS HAVEN'T ALWAYS LOOKED THE WAY THEY DO TODAY.

Over the years, strange events have come and gone from the Olympics, including Literature, Architecture, and Music.

9. FOR MANY YEARS, IT WAS FROWNED UPON—AND SOMETIMES ILLEGAL—FOR WOMEN TO WEAR PANTS.

In fact, women were not allowed to wear pants on the floor of the US Senate until 1993.

10. THE CLEANING PRODUCT LYSOL WAS ONCE MARKETED AS A CONTRACEPTIVE.

Unfortunately, the product was damaging to flesh and wasn't even particularly effective as contraception.

11. INTERRACIAL MARRIAGE DID NOT BECOME FULLY LEGAL IN THE UNITED STATES UNTIL 1967.

That's depressingly recent....

12. BEYONCÉ USED TO CHARGE HER PARENTS' FRIENDS $5 TO WATCH HER PERFORM AS A KIDDO.

If only her tickets were still so affordable.

· 13 ·

IN 1908, NEW YORK CITY PASSED AN ORDINANCE THAT BANNED WOMEN FROM SMOKING IN PUBLIC.

The law lasted just two weeks before the backlash prompted the mayor to veto it.

• 14 •

THE POPE ONCE WROTE AN EROTIC NOVEL.

The Tale of Two Lovers was written in 1444 by Aeneas Sylvius Piccolomini, who would later become Pope Pius II. You can still read the book today!

15. IN THE 19TH CENTURY, ONE OF THE MOST POPULAR SPORTS IN THE WORLD WAS PEDESTRIANISM...BETTER KNOWN AS "COMPETITIVE WALKING."

16. THERE IS NO HISTORICAL EVIDENCE THAT THE VIKINGS ACTUALLY WORE HORNED HELMETS.

17. GENGHIS KHAN SIRED CHILDREN SO PROLIFICALLY AND OVER SO GREAT AN AREA THAT ROUGHLY 1 IN 200 MEN ALIVE TODAY IS BELIEVED TO BE A DESCENDANT OF THE KHAGAN.

18. THE NATIONAL SCHOOL LUNCH PROGRAM IN THE UNITED STATES WAS CREATED FOLLOWING WWII AS A WAY TO ENSURE THAT, IF THE MILITARY DRAFT WERE EVER NECESSARY AGAIN, THE DRAFT POOL WOULD BE HEALTHIER AND MORE ABLE-BODIED.

19. MOZART WASN'T JUST A GENIUS; HE COULD HAVE FUN TOO.

He once wrote a canon titled "Leck mich im Arsch"—German for "Lick me in the arse." Historians believe it was jokingly written for the entertainment of his friends.

20. THE US GOVERNMENT INTENTIONALLY POISONED ALCOHOL DURING PROHIBITION, IN WHAT WAS THEN CALLED THE "NOBLE EXPERIMENT."

The goal was to discourage the illegal consumption of alcohol, but some estimate that the program's death toll was as high as 10,000.

21. FLORENCE GRIFFITH JOYNER IS CONSIDERED THE FASTEST WOMAN OF ALL TIME, WITH RECORDS FROM 1988 IN THE 100- AND 200-METER DASHES THAT STILL STAND TODAY.

22. THE TERM "MAVERICK" COMES FROM A REAL PERSON: SAMUEL MAVERICK WAS A 19TH-CENTURY RANCHER WHO REFUSED TO BRAND HIS CATTLE, AND HIS NAME EVENTUALLY BECAME SYNONYMOUS WITH INDEPENDENT THINKING.

23. NO WITCHES WERE BURNED AT THE STAKE DURING THE SALEM WITCH TRIALS.

Many people convicted of witchcraft were killed by hanging, but there is no evidence that any were burned at the stake.

24. DURING THE 19TH AND 20TH CENTURIES, "HUMAN ZOOS" WERE NOT UNCOMMON IN WESTERN COUNTRIES.

At these locations, humans from other cultures were displayed in their so-called "primitive" states. Thankfully, the trend eventually died out.

• 25 •

DURING THE GREAT DEPRESSION, PEOPLE MADE CLOTHING OUT OF THINGS LIKE POTATO OR FLOUR SACKS.

This led companies to make their sacks more colorful to attract "fashionable" buyers.

• 26 •

COWBOY HATS WEREN'T ACTUALLY ALL THAT POPULAR IN THE AMERICAN WEST.

In fact, the most commonly worn hat at the time was the bowler. Still, we can all agree that Clint Eastwood would be much less cool in a bowler hat.

27. IN AD 897, POPE STEPHEN VI EXHUMED THE CORPSE OF HIS PREDECESSOR, PUT IT ON TRIAL, AND RE-EXECUTED IT. THE INCIDENT BECAME KNOWN AS THE "CADAVER SYNOD."

28. IN 1967, KATHRINE SWITZER BECAME THE FIRST WOMAN TO BE A REGISTERED RUNNER AND RUN THE BOSTON MARATHON, FIVE YEARS BEFORE WOMEN WERE OFFICIALLY ALLOWED TO RACE.

29. IN THE 15TH CENTURY, MANY OF THOSE WHO FEARED WITCHES BELIEVED THEY HAD A HABIT OF STEALING MEN'S PENISES AND KEEPING THEM AS "PETS."

30. THE MYTH OF ATLANTIS ORIGINATES WITH THE PHILOSOPHER PLATO, BUT HE NEVER ACTUALLY BELIEVED IN IT; HIS TALE OF ATLANTIS WAS JUST PART OF AN ALLEGORY.

31. THE INVENTION OF GIN LED TO A PERIOD KNOWN IN ENGLAND AS THE "GIN CRAZE."

Gin was so cheap that a significant portion of the population was intoxicated almost all the time, and the government eventually had to step in and regulate the industry.

32. IN THE EARLY 1930S, A MAN NAMED PLENNIE WINGO PERFORMED A STRANGE FEAT: HE WALKED BACKWARD FOR 8,000 MILES, FROM CALIFORNIA TO ISTANBUL.

33. BETWEEN 1900 AND 1960, THE RATE OF LEFT-HANDEDNESS INCREASED FROM ABOUT 2% OF PEOPLE TO 12%.

The reason is simple: left-handedness became less socially stigmatized over time, leading lefties to feel more comfortable being themselves.

34. THOUGH ASSIGNED MALE AT BIRTH, THE CHEVALIER D'ÉON (A CELEBRATED SOLDIER AND SPY BORN IN 1728) SUCCESSFULLY PETITIONED BOTH THE FRENCH AND ENGLISH GOVERNMENTS TO BE LEGALLY RECOGNIZED AS A WOMAN.

It is one of the earliest known examples of legal transgender recognition.

35. BETWEEN THE 17TH CENTURY AND THE 19TH CENTURY, DIVORCE WAS SO EXPENSIVE IN ENGLAND THAT ONLY THE RICH COULD AFFORD IT.

The poor often had to resort to "wife selling," which is exactly what it sounds like.

36. AGNÈS SOREL, AN OFFICIALLY RECOGNIZED "ROYAL MISTRESS" OF FRANCE'S KING CHARLES VII, MADE WAVES IN THE ROYAL COURT WITH HER FASHION CHOICES; NAMELY, SHE HAD A HABIT OF UNLACING HER BODICE TO LEAVE ONE OR BOTH BREASTS EXPOSED.

• 37 •

GLADIATOR SWEAT WAS
HIGHLY SOUGHT AFTER IN
ROME, AND WAS OFTEN
MIXED INTO PERFUMES AND
USED AS AN APHRODISIAC.

· 38 ·

HUNDREDS OF YEARS AGO, IT WAS COMMONLY BELIEVED THAT SHEEP GREW ON TREES AND WERE THEREFORE PLANTS.

39. JAMES JOYCE, AUTHOR OF SUCH CLASSIC WORKS AS *ULYSSES* AND *A PORTRAIT OF THE ARTIST AS A YOUNG MAN*, HAD A VERY SPECIFIC FETISH: HE WAS OBSESSED WITH HIS WIFE'S FARTS, AND WROTE HER LONG, DETAILED LETTERS ABOUT THEM THAT WERE DISCOVERED AFTER HIS DEATH.

40. IN 1770, A BILL PROPOSING THAT WOMEN USING MAKEUP SHOULD BE PUNISHED FOR WITCHCRAFT WAS PUT FORWARD TO THE BRITISH PARLIAMENT.

The use of makeup was frowned upon during this period for the effect it would have on men, and women who were thought to be luring men in with scents, makeup, wigs, or other cosmetics were thought to be performing the Devil's work by inciting lustfulness. Even the Queen took a hard stance on makeup, calling it "impolite."

41. POPE BENEDICT IX WAS THE ONLY PERSON TO SERVE AS POPE MORE THAN ONCE—AND HE DID IT THREE SEPARATE TIMES.

The second time, he stepped down in exchange for money, becoming the only pope to sell his position.

42. THE POLICE HAVEN'T BEEN AROUND AS LONG AS YOU MIGHT THINK: THE FIRST PUBLICLY FUNDED POLICE DEPARTMENT IN THE UNITED STATES WAS FORMED IN BOSTON IN 1838, WITH DEPARTMENTS IN NYC AND PHILADELPHIA FOLLOWING IN 1844 AND 1854.

43. WHILE BETSY ROSS DID SEW FLAGS, NO OFFICIAL DOCUMENTATION HAS BEEN FOUND TO CONFIRM THAT BETSY ROSS WAS RESPONSIBLE FOR CREATING THE VERY FIRST AMERICAN FLAG, ALTHOUGH IT IS CONCEIVABLE.

Some historians attribute the design of the first flag to Francis Hopkinson, who sought payment from the Board of Admiralty in 1780 for his design of the "flag of the United States of America." However, his petition for payment was denied on the grounds that "he was not the only one consulted" on the design.

44. ONE OF P. T. BARNUM'S EXHIBITS WAS AN ELDERLY BLACK WOMAN NAMED JOICE HETH, WHOM HE CLAIMED WAS THE 161-YEAR-OLD FORMER NURSE OF GEORGE WASHINGTON.

When she died, things took an even more grotesque turn; he hired a doctor to perform a live autopsy on stage.

45. CLAUDETTE COLVIN REFUSED TO GIVE UP HER BUS SEAT TO A WHITE WOMAN 9 MONTHS BEFORE ROSA PARKS DID THE SAME.

But because she was unmarried and pregnant, civil rights activists did not think she was an appropriate person to publicly champion the movement.

46. WHILE THERE IS (OBVIOUSLY) NO WRITTEN RECORD, RESEARCHERS BELIEVE HUMAN LANGUAGE ONLY DATES BACK AROUND 50,000 TO 100,000 YEARS. THAT'S NOT A LOT OF TIME, HISTORICALLY SPEAKING!

· 47 ·

COFFEE WAS OFTEN REFERRED TO AS "THE DEVIL'S DRINK" UNTIL POPE CLEMENT VIII FINALLY TRIED IT.

He liked it so much he "baptized" it and helped popularize it in Europe.

48. AMERICAN SINGER KELLY CLARKSON CAUSED AN UPROAR IN 2012 WHEN, AT AN AUCTION, SHE PURCHASED A GOLD AND TURQUOISE RING OWNED BY JANE AUSTEN FOR £152,450.

Britain's culture minister put an immediate export ban on the ring, preventing Clarkson from taking it home to the United States. Two years later, Clarkson withdrew her ownership.

49. ONE REASON GREEK SCULPTURES DON'T TEND TO BE "WELL ENDOWED" IS THAT THE ANCIENT GREEKS BELIEVED SMALL PENISES WERE MORE ELEGANT AND MODEST, WHILE LARGE PENISES WERE ASSOCIATED WITH LUSTFUL BARBARISM.

50. MOST PEOPLE THINK OF VICTORIAN ENGLAND AS A STUFFY AND FORMAL TIME, BUT ONE POPULAR FASHION TREND BUCKS THAT PERCEPTION: VICTORIAN WOMEN REGULARLY HAD THEIR NIPPLES PIERCED.

51. THE CHURCH OF ENGLAND WAS STARTED BY KING HENRY VIII.

What made him break from the Roman Catholic Church? The pope's refusal to grant him a divorce.

52. GREEK AND ROMAN STATUES WEREN'T ALWAYS WHITE MARBLE.

They were originally painted, often in bright colors, but faded to white over time. The image we have today of Athens and Rome as austere and colorless is simply untrue.

53. GREEK PLAYWRIGHT AESCHYLUS, OFTEN CONSIDERED THE "FATHER OF TRAGEDY," WAS REPORTEDLY KILLED WHEN AN EAGLE MISTOOK HIS BALD HEAD FOR A ROCK AND DROPPED A TURTLE ON IT.

A fitting death for the master of tragedy!

54. NO ONE IS EXACTLY SURE WHO BUILT THE GREAT SPHINX.

In fact, we're not even sure when it was built; estimates range from 2500 BC to 7000 BC.

55. IN INDIA AND NEPAL, THE PRACTICE OF WIDOW BURNING (SATI) OCCURRED WHEN WOMEN BURNED THEMSELVES ALIVE ON THEIR HUSBANDS' FUNERAL PYRES AS A SIGN OF DEVOTION AND LOVE.

It was meant to be a voluntary act, but occasionally women were drugged or pushed into the fire. In Nepal in 1920, legislation was enforced that abolished the act of sati. In India today, sati is still practiced, but it has been largely confined to Rajasthan, with a few instances in the Indo-Gangetic Plain.

56. THE POPULARITY OF THE *MONA LISA* ONLY SKYROCKETED AFTER THE PAINTING WAS STOLEN BY AN ITALIAN HANDYMAN WHO WANTED TO RETURN THE PAINTING TO ITALY.

· 57 ·

DURING MAO'S "GREAT LEAP FORWARD," CHINA WAGED WAR ON SPARROWS, WHICH WERE KNOWN TO EAT THE GRAIN GROWN BY FARMERS.

Unfortunately, they also ate locusts, and the campaign against the sparrows was so successful that locust populations exploded for years, destroying vastly more crops than the sparrows ever had.

58. JUST BEFORE HE BECAME THE FIRST MAN IN SPACE, YURI GAGARIN RELIEVED HIMSELF ON THE WHEEL OF THE BUS THAT HAD DRIVEN HIM TO THE LAUNCHING PAD.

Today, urinating on the wheel of the bus is still a launch-day tradition among Russian cosmonauts.

59. ALFRED NOBEL CREATED THE NOBEL PEACE PRIZE OUT OF GUILT.

After a newspaper mistakenly published an obituary for the very-much-still-alive Nobel which referred to him as "The Merchant of Death," he rewrote his will to create a foundation to promote more peaceful and meaningful endeavors.

60. PROSTITUTION IS ILLEGAL IN IRAN, SO THE PRACTICE OF "TEMPORARY MARRIAGE" (A SHORT-TERM RELATIONSHIP THAT AUTOMATICALLY EXPIRES) IS OFTEN USED AS A LOOPHOLE.

61. DURING HER FIRST MISSIONARY POST AT ST. MARY'S HIGH SCHOOL IN CALCUTTA, MOTHER TERESA TAUGHT HER PUPILS BY WRITING IN THE MUD WITH STICKS BECAUSE SHE WAS NOT GIVEN ANY RESOURCES OR SUPPLIES.

62. IN 1985, THE PHILADELPHIA POLICE DROPPED TWO BOMBS ON A HOUSE OCCUPIED BY BLACK ACTIVISTS, AND THE FIRE DEPARTMENT REFUSED TO PUT OUT THE FLAMES.

The MOVE Bombing (as it came to be known) left 11 dead and another 250 homeless, but is largely unknown outside of Philadelphia.

63. WHEN THE AUSTRALIAN CITY OF MELBOURNE WAS FIRST FOUNDED, IT WAS NAMED "BATMANIA" AFTER ONE OF ITS ORIGINAL SETTLERS, JOHN BATMAN.

64. THE "HIGH FIVE" WASN'T INVENTED UNTIL 1977, WHEN LOS ANGELES DODGERS PLAYERS GLENN BURKE AND DUSTY BAKER SPONTANEOUSLY SLAPPED HANDS TO CELEBRATE THE HOME RUN BAKER HAD JUST HIT.

65. AFTER THE FRENCH REVOLUTION, THE FRENCH ATTEMPTED TO INSTITUTE "DECIMAL TIME," WHICH INCLUDED A 10-HOUR DAY WITH 100 MINUTES PER HOUR AND 100 SECONDS PER MINUTE.

It did not last.

66. WHEN THE PENTAGON WAS CONSTRUCTED, RACIAL SEGREGATION WAS STILL IN PLACE.

As a result, the Pentagon today has twice as many bathrooms as it technically needs.

67. IN 1847, THE CHOCTAW NATION SENT $170 TO HELP THE IRISH DURING THE IRISH POTATO FAMINE.

More than 150 years later, the Irish responded by sending aid to Native American tribes during the COVID-19 pandemic.

68. AS WITH AMERICAN HISTORY, RUSSIAN HISTORY CONTAINS PERIODS WHERE LARGE NUMBERS OF PEOPLE WERE ACCUSED OF WITCHCRAFT.

The difference? In Russia, the vast majority of accused witches were men.

• 69 •

ACCORDING TO LEGEND, UPON THE COMPLETION OF ST. BASIL'S CATHEDRAL, IVAN THE TERRIBLE BLINDED THE ARCHITECTS SO THEY COULD NEVER DESIGN ANYTHING SO BEAUTIFUL AGAIN.

70. THE WORLD'S FIRST NOVEL, *THE TALE OF GENJI*, WAS PUBLISHED IN JAPAN AROUND AD 1000 BY FEMALE AUTHOR MURASAKI SHIKIBU.

It is still revered today for its masterful observations about court life and has been translated into dozens of languages.

71. AT THE TIME OF THE AMERICAN REVOLUTION, ONLY AN ESTIMATED 10%-20% OF THE COLONIAL POPULATION BELONGED TO A CHURCH (THOUGH A MAJORITY DID IDENTIFY AS CHRISTIAN).

72. IN THE EARLY 1900S, MANY WOMEN TOOK TO WEARING "HOBBLE SKIRTS," WHICH WERE HEMMED SO NARROWLY THAT THEY COULD ONLY TAKE THE TINIEST OF STEPS.

The fad died out after the skirts were responsible for multiple deaths.

73. THE ROMANS USED A PLANT CALLED SILPHIUM AS A NATURAL CONTRACEPTIVE.

In fact, they used it so much that the plant went extinct.

74. GLADIATORS DIDN'T ACTUALLY DIE VERY OFTEN.

They were expensive to train and usually received excellent medical care. Most of the deaths in the arena were not gladiators, but condemned prisoners or other unwilling victims sent out to fight them.

75. THE PHRASE "MAD AS A HATTER" ORIGINATES WITH THE FACT THAT THE CHEMICALS USED IN HAT MAKING DURING THE 18TH AND 19TH CENTURIES HAD A SEVERELY DAMAGING EFFECT ON THE MENTAL WELL-BEING OF HATMAKERS.

76. IN THE LATE 1400S, A BUDDHIST MONK NAMED DRUKPA KUNLEY BECAME KNOWN FOR "BLESSING" WOMEN THROUGH SEXUAL INTERCOURSE—SO MUCH SO THAT HIS MEMBER IS STILL REFERRED TO AS THE "THUNDERBOLT OF FLAMING WISDOM."

77. SAMURAI EXISTED IN JAPAN MUCH MORE RECENTLY THAN YOU MIGHT EXPECT: THE SO-CALLED "AGE OF THE SAMURAI" LASTED FROM 1185 TO 1868.

78. THE IMMACULATE CONCEPTION DID NOT ACTUALLY BECOME OFFICIAL CATHOLIC DOCTRINE UNTIL 1854.

79. DESPITE ITS INCREDIBLE POPULARITY TODAY, SALMON WAS NOT USED IN JAPANESE SUSHI UNTIL AS RECENTLY AS THE 1990S.

80. THROUGHOUT EUROPEAN HISTORY, IT WAS CUSTOMARY FOR FRIENDS AND FAMILY TO STAND AS WITNESSES OF THE CONSUMMATION OF A MARRIAGE.

81. TRUE OR FALSE: BENJAMIN FRANKLIN PROPOSED MAKING THE TURKEY THE NATIONAL BIRD, RATHER THAN THE BALD EAGLE.

False. Franklin favorably compared the turkey to the eagle in a letter to his daughter, which gave birth to the myth. However, he never proposed making it the national bird.

82. TRUE OR FALSE: ALMOST 1 OUT OF EVERY 100 PEOPLE IN THE UNITED STATES IS IN A PRISON OR JAIL.

True. Roughly 0.7% of the US population is incarcerated at any given time. The United States makes up just 4% of the world's population, but contains 20% of its incarcerated persons.

83. TRUE OR FALSE: AN ORSON WELLES AUDIO DRAMA BASED ON THE H. G. WELLS NOVEL *THE WAR OF THE WORLDS* CAUSED MASS PANIC WHEN LISTENERS MISTOOK IT FOR AN ACTUAL NEWS BROADCAST.

False. This legend doesn't have much basis in fact. While it's true that some people probably believed it, the number was almost certainly very small.

84. TRUE OR FALSE: POPE CALLIXTUS III EXCOMMUNICATED HALLEY'S COMET.

False. While the pope expressed fear and concern about the comet's appearance, the tales that he invoked his papal authority against it are largely exaggerated.

85. TRUE OR FALSE: CHARLIE CHAPLIN ONCE ENTERED A CHARLIE CHAPLIN LOOK-ALIKE CONTEST AND CAME IN 20TH PLACE.

False. The rumor is popular for obvious reasons—it's a great story! But Chaplin himself denied it, and it seems like the sort of thing he'd boast about if it were true.

86. TRUE OR FALSE: CHARLES DICKENS'S BOOKS ARE SO LONG BECAUSE HE WAS PAID BY THE WORD.

False. Though it would certainly explain a lot, this is just an urban legend.

87. TRUE OR FALSE: CHOKER NECKLACES ORIGINATED AROUND THE FRENCH REVOLUTION AS A SYMBOL OF SUPPORT FOR THE GUILLOTINE.

False. It's a popular rumor, but there are portraits of women wearing chokers long before that—including Anne Boleyn.

88. TRUE OR FALSE: A TEENAGE GIRL STRUCK OUT BOTH BABE RUTH AND LOU GEHRIG IN ONE GAME.

True. In 1931, 17-year-old pitcher Jackie Mitchell made baseball history when she struck out Babe Ruth and Lou Gehrig during an exhibition game against the Yankees.

89. TRUE OR FALSE: CROCODILE DUNG WAS A COMMON FORM OF BIRTH CONTROL IN ANCIENT EGYPT.

True. Interestingly, the acidic properties of crocodile dung mean that it was probably at least partially effective.

· 90 ·

TRUE OR FALSE: HIGH-HEELED SHOES WERE ORIGINALLY WORN BY MEN.

True. High heels were first worn in Persia by men who wanted to appear taller. They then brought the fad to France, and it spread from there.

• 91 •

TRUE OR FALSE: THE CROISSANT WAS FIRST CREATED TO COMMEMORATE A VICTORY OVER THE OTTOMAN EMPIRE.

True. Many historians believe the croissant was created not in France, but in Vienna—and its shape mimicked the flag of the Ottoman forces defeated during the Battle of Vienna.

92. TRUE OR FALSE: THE IRON MAIDEN WAS ONE OF THE MOST COMMONLY USED TORTURE DEVICES IN THE MIDDLE AGES.

False. In fact, there is no evidence that the Iron Maiden existed before the 19th century, and its use as a torture device is generally considered to be a myth.

93. TRUE OR FALSE: HISTORIANS ESTIMATE THAT 25% OF THE COWBOYS IN THE AMERICAN WEST WERE BLACK.

True. While actors like Clint Eastwood and John Wayne personify the archetypal cowboy in media, as many as one in four cowboys was likely Black.

94. TRUE OR FALSE: IN 1994, THE TOP MARGINAL TAX RATE IN THE UNITED STATES WAS 94%.

True. While the wealthy often complain about being taxed unfairly, today's top marginal rate is just 37%!

95. TRUE OR FALSE: AFTER THE CIVIL WAR, MISSISSIPPI WAS THE FIRST OF THE FORMER CONFEDERATE STATES TO ABOLISH SLAVERY.

False. In fact, Mississippi didn't officially ratify the 13th Amendment until 2013.

96. TRUE OR FALSE: THOMAS JEFFERSON WROTE HIS OWN VERSION OF THE NEW TESTAMENT OF THE BIBLE.

True. Jefferson's version omitted references to Jesus's miracles (including his resurrection) and other elements that he believed were too fantastical to be true.

97. TRUE OR FALSE: CANADA ONCE DECLARED A MATERNITY WARD TO BE "EXTRATERRITORIAL LAND."

True. During WWII, the royal family of the Netherlands fled to Canada. The princess was pregnant, and it was important that the child be a Dutch citizen, not a Canadian one.

98. TRUE OR FALSE: ADOLF HITLER IS CONSIDERED A SAINT IN THE PALMARIAN CHRISTIAN CHURCH.

False. The Palmarian Christian Church has some unusual beliefs, which probably sparked the internet hoax claiming the church had canonized Hitler. It is not true.

99. TRUE OR FALSE: AT ONE TIME, BLUE DYE WAS MORE VALUABLE THAN GOLD.

True. Blue dye has historically been difficult to make, due to the rarity of blue pigments in nature. Ultramarine, one of the most popular sources of blue pigment, was often more valuable than gold.

• 100 •

TRUE OR FALSE: IT WAS, AT ONE POINT, LEGAL TO USE THE US POSTAL SERVICE TO SEND CHILDREN THROUGH THE MAIL.

True. From 1913 to 1915, a number of crafty families used the USPS as a transportation service for their children. Eventually, stricter rules for what could and could not be mailed were established.

Science & Invention

It's often said that genius and madness are different sides of the same coin. But if history is any indication, they might just be the same side of that coin. Have you ever heard of Franz Reichelt, the French tailor who leapt off the Eiffel Tower with a parachute of his own design? Or the time Nikola Tesla cured Mark Twain's constipation by having him stand on a vibrating disc? Yes, scientists and inventors are often eccentric—and the most unbelievable part of all might just be how often their wild ideas work!

1. "ELK CLONER," ONE OF THE FIRST KNOWN SELF-SPREADING COMPUTER VIRUSES, WAS CREATED AS A JOKE BY A 15-YEAR-OLD KID.

2. FAMED ASTRONOMER TYCHO BRAHE WAS KNOWN FOR WEARING A GOLDEN PROSTHETIC TO COVER UP A MISSING CHUNK OF HIS NOSE.

How did he lose that chunk? In a drunken duel with a cousin over who was better at math.

3. CHARLES DARWIN DIDN'T JUST STUDY THE ANIMALS OF THE WORLD—HE ATE THEM AS WELL.

Darwin was known for his willingness to eat just about anything, from tortoise bladders to giant rodents.

4. KETCHUP WAS ONCE SOLD AS MEDICINE.

5. CONTACT LENSES WERE INVENTED A LOT EARLIER THAN YOU PROBABLY THINK: THE FIRST ONES HIT THE MARKET IN THE LATE 1800S, THOUGH THEY ADMITTEDLY LOOKED A LOT DIFFERENT FROM THE LENSES OF TODAY.

6. BEFORE ALARM CLOCKS WERE INVENTED, PEOPLE IN SOME EUROPEAN COUNTRIES COULD HIRE A "KNOCKER-UPPER" TO KNOCK ON THEIR BEDROOM WINDOW AND WAKE THEM WHEN IT WAS TIME FOR WORK.

7. BECAUSE PEOPLE WERE NOT ACCUSTOMED TO THE SPEED OF TRAINS, MANY VICTORIANS BELIEVED THAT RIDING ON A TRAIN COULD TRIGGER IMMEDIATE, VIOLENT MADNESS.

8. IN THE 1960S, NASA FUNDED AN EXPERIMENT TO STUDY DOLPHINS...AND A FEMALE RESEARCHER FELL IN LOVE WITH ONE OF THE DOLPHINS AND BEGAN A SEXUAL RELATIONSHIP WITH IT.

9. THE CAN OPENER WAS INVENTED ALMOST 50 YEARS AFTER THE CAN.

Until then, people mostly opened their cans with a hammer and chisel.

· 10 ·

BEFORE THE INVENTION
OF TOILET PAPER, EARLY
AMERICANS USED CORNCOBS
TO CLEAN THEMSELVES.

• 11 •

ONE WOMAN, VIOLET JESSOP, MIRACULOUSLY SURVIVED NOT JUST THE SINKING OF THE *TITANIC*, BUT ITS SISTER SHIP THE *BRITANNIC* AS WELL.

12. HEROIN WAS ONCE ADDED TO MEDICINES AS A COUGH SUPPRESSANT.

13. RADIATION WAS ONCE BELIEVED TO BE A HEALTH AID—SO MUCH SO THAT RADIOACTIVE SUBSTANCES LIKE RADON WERE ADDED TO WATER AND OTHER CONSUMABLES AND SOLD AS HEALTH TONICS.

The results were predictably catastrophic.

14. TWENTIETH-CENTURY DOCTOR JOHN ROMULUS BRINKLEY DIDN'T JUST HAVE AN INTERESTING NAME—HE HAD AN INTERESTING SPECIALTY.

Brinkley became known for transplanting goat testicles into humans, which he fraudulently claimed would boost virility and fertility.

15. DURING THE 16TH AND 17TH CENTURIES, HUMAN FLESH WAS OFTEN INCORPORATED INTO MEDICINAL RECIPES.

Stolen Egyptian mummies were a particularly prized ingredient.

16. THE FAX MACHINE IS OLDER THAN YOU MIGHT EXPECT—IT WAS PATENTED BY ALEXANDER BAIN IN 1843!

17. WE MAY TALK ABOUT WATSON AND CRICK'S DOUBLE-HELIX DISCOVERY IN SCIENCE CLASS, BUT BRITISH CHEMIST ROSALIND FRANKLIN IS THE ONE WHO REVEALED DNA'S STRUCTURE.

18. ASTRONAUT JIM LEBLANC WAS ALMOST KILLED WHEN THE EARLY SPACE-SUIT DESIGN HE WAS TESTING FAILED AND EXPOSED HIM TO ALMOST TOTAL VACUUM.

19. MATHEMATICIAN KATHERINE JOHNSON'S MATHEMATICAL COMPUTATIONS HELPED LAUNCH JOHN GLENN INTO ORBIT AND SEND APOLLO 11 TO THE MOON.

She was so good at what she did, NASA would have her double-check equations done by the computers.

20. IN THE 1960S, THE SCIENTIFIC WORLD BECAME OBSESSED WITH "POLYWATER," A "NEW FORM OF WATER" CREATED BY THE SOVIETS.

Later experiments revealed that polywater was just...dirty water.

21. IN 1894, AN AUSTRIAN SCIENTIST NAMED HANNS HÖRBIGER PUT FORTH A NEW THEORY: THAT PLANETS, MOONS, AND ALL OTHER CELESTIAL OBJECTS ARE MADE OF ICE.

The theory gained enough steam that high-ranking Nazis including Hitler and Himmler were known to be adherents to this "World Ice Doctrine."

• 22 •

BECAUSE BLOOD TRANSFUSIONS WERE SO RISKY, DOCTORS IN THE 1800S TRIED USING A NUMBER OF "BLOOD SUBSTITUTES."

One of the most popular was cow's milk, which...was not very successful.

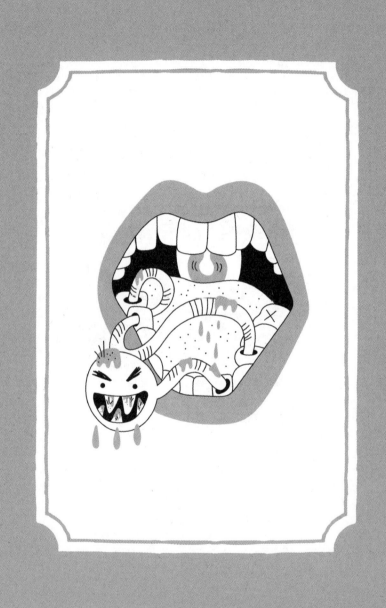

· 23 ·

EARLY DENTISTS BELIEVED CAVITIES WERE CAUSED BY "TOOTH WORMS," WHICH LIVED INSIDE THE TEETH AND ATE THEM AWAY.

This was believed well into the 1700s.

24. IN 1903, MARY ANDERSON WAS GRANTED A PATENT FOR THE WINDSHIELD WIPER.

It would become standard equipment on cars by 1916.

25. ONE OF THE EARLIEST TREATMENTS FOR SYPHILIS WAS...MALARIA.

While there was no cure for syphilis, doctors could treat malaria, and the high fever caused by malaria could kill the syphilis-causing bacteria in the body.

26. THE LAST KNOWN NATURAL CASE OF SMALLPOX WAS RECORDED IN 1977....BUT IN 1978, A MEDICAL PHOTOGRAPHER NAMED JANET PARKER DIED FROM THE DISEASE WHEN IT ESCAPED A UNIVERSITY TESTING LAB.

She was the last known person to die from smallpox.

27. NANCY JOHNSON INVENTED A HAND-OPERATED ICE-CREAM MAKER IN 1983, WHOSE DESIGN IS STILL USED TODAY!

28. THE INVENTORS OF INSULIN SOLD THE PATENT FOR THE DRUG FOR $1 BECAUSE THEY WANTED IT TO BE AFFORDABLE FOR EVERYONE.

Unfortunately, it hasn't exactly worked out that way.

29. THE "IMMORTAL" HELA CELLS OFTEN USED IN BIOMEDICAL RESEARCH WERE TAKEN WITHOUT PERMISSION FROM AFRICAN AMERICAN PATIENT HENRIETTA LACKS AFTER SHE DIED FROM CERVICAL CANCER.

Over 110,000 publications have cited the use of HeLa cells between 1953 and 2018.

30. *PONG* WASN'T ACTUALLY THE FIRST VIDEO GAME: ALL THE WAY BACK IN 1947, A MAN NAMED THOMAS GOLDSMITH DEVELOPED WHAT HE CALLED A "CATHODE-RAY TUBE AMUSEMENT DEVICE" THAT SIMULATED A MISSILE-LAUNCHING GAME.

31. EXAMINING THE BODIES OF ANCIENT HUMANS HAS LED SCIENTISTS TO BELIEVE THAT EARLY FORMS OF "BRAIN SURGERY" WERE PRACTICED AS LONG AGO AS 5000 BC.

32. THE MICROWAVE WAS INVENTED COMPLETELY BY MISTAKE.

Percy Spencer, a radar researcher for Raytheon, paused next to a magnetron during an experiment and realized that the chocolate bar in his pocket was melting.

• 33 •

IN 1912, A FRENCH TAILOR NAMED FRANZ REICHELT LEAPT FROM THE TOP OF THE EIFFEL TOWER WEARING A HOMEMADE PARACHUTE OF HIS OWN DESIGN—DESPITE THE FACT THAT HE HAD NEVER SUCCESSFULLY TESTED IT.

Unfortunately, the parachute failed to open, leading to a predictable result.

· 34 ·

IN 1910, THE PANIC
SURROUNDING THE ARRIVAL
OF HALLEY'S COMET LED
TO A RASH OF SCAMS,
INCLUDING "COMET
UMBRELLAS" AND
"ANTICOMET PILLS."

35. AN AMERICAN DOCTOR NAMED STUBBINS FFIRTH ATTEMPTED TO PROVE THAT YELLOW FEVER WAS NOT CONTAGIOUS BY DRINKING THE VOMIT OF YELLOW FEVER PATIENTS.

He was also known to cover his body in their vomit, blood, and urine to further test his hypothesis.

36. IN 1503, A BAVARIAN KNIGHT NAMED GÖTZ VON BERLICHINGEN RECEIVED ONE OF THE EARLIEST FUNCTIONAL PROSTHETICS IN HISTORY: HE HAD A FALSE HAND MADE OF IRON THAT WAS CAPABLE OF GRIPPING A SWORD AND EVEN SHAKING A HAND.

37. NIKOLA TESLA ONCE REPORTEDLY CURED MARK TWAIN'S CONSTIPATION BY HAVING HIM STAND ON A VIBRATING METAL DISC.

It took less than two minutes for Twain to shout for the bathroom!

38. FRANCIS CRICK, ONE OF THE SCIENTISTS WHO HELPED DISCOVER THE STRUCTURE OF DNA, ALSO BELIEVED THAT LIFE ON EARTH ORIGINATED WITH THE HELP OF ALIENS.

39. THE FIRST ANIMALS SENT TO SPACE WERE FRUIT FLIES, FOR A VERY IMPORTANT REASON: FRUIT FLIES SHARE ABOUT 75% OF THE DISEASE-CAUSING GENES PRESENT IN HUMANS, WHICH MADE THEM AN EXCELLENT (AND EASY-TO-STUDY) STAND-IN FOR HUMANS.

40. MARIE CURIE'S BELONGINGS WERE SO IRRADIATED THAT NEARLY 100 YEARS AFTER HER DEATH, THEY ARE STILL STORED IN LEAD-LINED BOXES.

They will continue to be too radioactive to handle for another 1,500 years.

41. ELLEN OCHOA ISN'T JUST AN INVENTOR OF OPTICAL DEVICES FOR NASA—SHE'S ALSO A PIONEER.

In 1993, she embarked on a nine-day mission to space aboard the *Discovery* space shuttle, making her the first female Hispanic astronaut.

42. THE FIRST TALKING BABY DOLL WAS CREATED BY THOMAS EDISON IN 1890, AND IT WAS EVERY BIT AS CREEPY AS YOU MIGHT IMAGINE.

43. THE FIRST LOCAL ANESTHETIC TO BE DISCOVERED AND USED FOR MEDICAL PURPOSES WAS...COCAINE.

44. THE SYMBOLS WE CALL "ARABIC NUMERALS" TODAY WERE ACTUALLY INVENTED IN INDIA—BUT IT WAS ARABS WHO BROUGHT THEM TO THE WEST.

45. IN THE 19TH CENTURY, A MAN NAMED HARVEY ADAMS SET THE TEA-DRINKING WORLD ON FIRE WHEN HE INVENTED THE "MUSTACHE CUP"—A TEACUP WITH A SMALL LEDGE INSIDE TO PROTECT THE DRINKER'S MUSTACHE.

· 46 ·

THE CHOCOLATE CHIP
COOKIE WAS INVENTED
BY DIETITIAN RUTH
WAKEFIELD, WHO LATER
SOLD THE RECIPE TO
NESTLÉ IN EXCHANGE FOR
A LIFETIME SUPPLY OF
CHOCOLATE.

47. HUMANS LANDED ON THE MOON JUST 66 YEARS AFTER THE WRIGHT BROTHERS' FIRST FLIGHT.

48. DURING THE 1920S, A RUSSIAN RESEARCHER NAMED ILYA IVANOV SPENT YEARS ATTEMPTING TO CREATE HUMAN-CHIMPANZEE HYBRIDS USING ARTIFICIAL INSEMINATION.

He was, uh, not successful.

49. ELDORADO JONES, FAMOUS FOR HER NICKNAME "IRON WOMAN," WAS THE OWNER OF A METALWORKING FACTORY WHERE ONLY WOMEN AGED OVER 40 WERE EMPLOYED.

And while she never got the funding to manufacture it, she received the credit for being the inventor of the airplane engine muffler in 1917.

50. WHEN ELECTRICITY WAS FIRST INSTALLED IN THE WHITE HOUSE IN 1891, BENJAMIN HARRISON, THE PRESIDENT AT THE TIME, REFUSED TO TOUCH ANY OF THE LIGHT SWITCHES HIMSELF OUT OF FEAR OF ELECTROCUTION.

51. THE FLAMETHROWER WAS INVENTED MUCH EARLIER THAN YOU MIGHT EXPECT: "GREEK FIRE" WAS A FLAMETHROWER-LIKE WEAPON USED BY THE GREEKS TO SET ENEMY SHIPS ON FIRE AS EARLY AS THE SEVENTH CENTURY.

52. SLICED BREAD WAS NOT INVENTED UNTIL 1928.

53. THE FIRST VENDING MACHINE WAS INVENTED BY HERO OF ALEXANDRIA DURING THE FIRST CENTURY.

When a coin was put into a slot, a small amount of holy water would be dispensed until the coin slid from its resting place.

54. THE CIGARETTE LIGHTER WAS INVENTED IN 1823...BUT THE MATCH WAS NOT INVENTED UNTIL 1826.

55. THE PEACEKEEPER AND NURSE ANN MOORE INVENTED THE CHILD CARRIER SNUGLI DURING THE 1960S.

While working during that time as a Peace Corps nurse in Togo, West Africa, she saw African mothers carrying their little ones in fabric slings securely tied to their backs. When she returned to the United States and had her own child, Moore and her mother developed a carrier that resembled those of mothers in Togo.

56. ETHAN ZUCKERMAN, THE INVENTOR OF POP-UP ADS, APOLOGIZED TO THE WORLD FOR HIS EXTREMELY ANNOYING CREATION IN 2014.

• 57 •

IN 1947, A NORWEGIAN
EXPLORER NAMED THOR
HEYERDAHL TRAVELED FROM
SOUTH AMERICA TO THE
POLYNESIAN ISLANDS ON
A WOODEN RAFT, SIMPLY
TO PROVE THAT ANCIENT
CULTURES COULD HAVE MADE
(AND LIKELY DID MAKE!) THE
SAME JOURNEY.

58. THE SWIVEL CHAIR WAS INVENTED BY…THOMAS JEFFERSON.

59. PERHAPS IT SHOULDN'T COME AS A SURPRISE THAT JOSEPH BRAMAH, THE MAN WHO INVENTED THE FLUSH TOILET, ALSO INVENTED THE BEER TAP.

The man knew how to move fluids!

60. LEO FENDER IS FAMOUS FOR DESIGNING THE TELECASTER AND STRATOCASTER GUITARS, DESPITE THE FACT THAT HE HAD NO IDEA HOW TO PLAY THE GUITAR HIMSELF.

61. WHEN THE INVENTOR OF THE FRISBEE DIED, HE WAS CREMATED AND, PER HIS INSTRUCTIONS, HIS ASHES WERE USED TO CREATE A FRISBEE.

62. JAMES BARRY WAS A RENOWNED IRISH SURGEON WHO PERFORMED ONE OF THE FIRST SUCCESSFUL CESAREAN SECTIONS.

After his death, it was revealed that he had been born Margaret Ann Bulkley, but lived as a man his entire adult life.

63. IN THE 1990S, A LINGUIST NAMED D'ARMOND SPEERS DECIDED TO CONDUCT AN EXPERIMENT ON THE LANGUAGE-ACQUISITION PROCESS BY ONLY SPEAKING KLINGON TO HIS SON FOR THE FIRST THREE YEARS OF HIS LIFE.

64. AS RECENTLY AS THE 1800S, MANY DOCTORS BELIEVED THAT HEALTH PROBLEMS IN WOMEN WERE CAUSED BY A "WANDERING WOMB."

They literally believed the uterus moved throughout the body, causing mayhem.

65. IN THE 1960S, A ZAMBIAN OFFICIAL NAMED EDWARD MAKUKA NKOLOSO ATTEMPTED TO CREATE A SPACE PROGRAM TO RIVAL THE UNITED STATES AND SOVIET UNION.

Rather than calling his explorers astronauts, he coined the term "Afronauts."

66. AMERICAN SCIENTIST NORMAN BORLAUG IS SAID TO HAVE SAVED MORE LIVES THAN ANYONE IN HISTORY: HE INVENTED SEVERAL STRAINS OF HIGH-YIELD WHEAT THAT MAY HAVE SAVED AS MANY AS A BILLION PEOPLE FROM STARVATION.

67. IN PARIS IN 1924, A CAR WITH A LARGE SHOVEL ATTACHED TO THE FRONT WAS TESTED. ITS PURPOSE? TO SAFELY PUSH JAYWALKERS OUT OF THE WAY.

Other variations on this idea were tested in the early 1900s as well, including a car with rollers on the front and a car which trapped pedestrians on the hood.

• 68 •

THE FIRST WOMAN IN SPACE WAS FROM THE SOVIET UNION.

Valentina Tereshkova was also the first
civilian in space when she lifted off in 1963.

69. FRITZ ZWICKY, THE DISCOVERER OF DARK MATTER, ALSO BELIEVED THAT LIGHT GOT "TIRED" WHEN TRAVELING GREAT DISTANCES AND THOUGHT THAT STARS CONTAINED SOMETHING HE DUBBED A "NUCLEAR GOBLIN."

He was an interesting character.

70. DESPITE BEING HAILED AS A HERO FOR CRACKING THE NAZI ENIGMA CODE, MATHEMATICIAN ALAN TURING WAS LATER PROSECUTED FOR HOMOSEXUAL ACTS AND CHEMICALLY CASTRATED AS PUNISHMENT.

71. JACK PARSONS WAS ONE OF THE INVENTORS OF THE ROCKET ENGINE AND IS CONSIDERED ONE OF THE FATHERS OF MODERN ROCKETRY.

He was also a student of famed occultist Aleister Crowley and a firm believer in magic.

72. A SCIENTIST NAMED DONALD UNGER SPENT 50 YEARS CRACKING THE KNUCKLES ON JUST ONE OF HIS HANDS TO PROVE THAT CRACKING KNUCKLES DOES NOT LEAD TO ARTHRITIS.

73. KURT GÖDEL, ONE OF THE MOST FAMOUS MATHEMATICIANS IN HISTORY, DEVELOPED EXTREME PARANOIA LATER IN LIFE AND REFUSED TO EAT ANY MEAL NOT PREPARED BY HIS WIFE.

When she was hospitalized and could no longer prepare his meals, he starved to death soon after.

74. IN 1911, A DOCTOR TRIED TO FIND THE MASS OF THE HUMAN SOUL BY MEASURING THE CHANGE IN MASS OF SIX HUMANS AT THE MOMENT OF THEIR DEATH.

75. THE TUNGUSKA EVENT WAS A MASSIVE DETONATION OVER SIBERIA CAUSED BY AN EXPLODING METEOR, BUT NIKOLA TESLA WAS BRIEFLY CONVINCED THAT HIS EXPERIMENT WITH A "DEATH RAY" HAD CAUSED THE DISASTER.

76. ALEXANDER GRAHAM BELL USED AN EARLY METAL DETECTOR OF HIS OWN DESIGN TO ATTEMPT TO SAVE PRESIDENT GARFIELD BY LOCATING THE BULLET LODGED IN HIS CHEST.

Unfortunately, the mattress Garfield was lying on contained metal springs, and the effort was unsuccessful, leading to Garfield's death.

77. PAUL REVERE WASN'T JUST A HERO OF THE REVOLUTIONARY WAR; HE WAS ALSO AMERICA'S FIRST FORENSIC DENTIST, AND HE USED HIS SKILLS TO IDENTIFY FALLEN SOLDIERS BASED ON THEIR DENTAL RECORDS.

78. PYTHAGORAS WAS ONE OF THE MOST FAMOUS MATHEMATICIANS OF ALL TIME, BUT HE WAS ALSO A CULT LEADER.

• 79 •

FRANK LLOYD WRIGHT WAS A FAMOUS ARCHITECT, BUT HIS SON JOHN SET HIS SIGHTS A LITTLE SMALLER—LITERALLY.

Perhaps taking inspiration from his father, John Lloyd Wright was the inventor of Lincoln Logs.

80. ÉVARISTE GALOIS, ONE OF THE FATHERS OF MODERN ALGEBRA, WAS HEAVILY INVOLVED IN THE FRENCH REVOLUTION, SPENT TIME IN JAIL, AND EVENTUALLY DIED IN A DUEL...AT AGE 20.

81. TRUE OR FALSE: TOBACCO-SMOKE ENEMAS WERE A POPULAR MEDICAL TREATMENT IN THE 18TH CENTURY.

True. It was used to treat stomach pain and other ailments—I'm not just blowing smoke up your ass!

82. TRUE OR FALSE: ON HIS DEATHBED, CHARLES DARWIN RENOUNCED EVOLUTION AND CONVERTED TO CHRISTIANITY.

False. While this rumor is still sometimes cited by creationists, there is no evidence that it actually happened.

83. TRUE OR FALSE: THE CHAINSAW WAS ORIGINALLY INVENTED TO HELP WITH CHILDBIRTH.

True. Unfortunately. It was hand cranked rather than gas powered, but early chainsaws were used to assist with the removal of the pelvic bone during difficult births. Ouch.

84. TRUE OR FALSE: THE STEAM ENGINE WAS INVENTED IN THE 1ST CENTURY BC.

True. The earliest steam engine was known as the "aeolipile," but it never amounted to much. It is not related to modern steam engines in any real way.

85. TRUE OR FALSE: ALBERT EINSTEIN FLUNKED HIS FOURTH-GRADE MATH CLASS.

False. It's a myth so pervasive that Einstein himself personally repudiated it during his life.

86. TRUE OR FALSE: EARLY DENTURES WERE MADE FROM THE TEETH OF DEAD MEN.

True. Everyone has heard tales of "wooden teeth," but early dentures often came from a different source.

87. TRUE OR FALSE: RADAR WAS ORIGINALLY INVENTED BY A RUSSIAN HERMIT, USING TIN CANS BENEATH A LAKE.

False. Actually, the British accidentally invented it while attempting to build a "death ray" during WWII.

88. TRUE OR FALSE: THE SAME CHEMICAL COMPOUND USED TO MAKE DEADLY MUSTARD GAS IN WWI WAS USED TO CREATE THE VERY FIRST CHEMOTHERAPY TREATMENTS.

True. By 1942, some good had finally come from the invention of mustard gas.

· 89 ·

TRUE OR FALSE: SCIENTISTS ONCE TURNED A LIVE CAT INTO A TELEPHONE.

True. In 1929, two Princeton University researchers used a cat's auditory nerve to create a telephone receiver. The cat survived (but was later killed in a different experiment).

· 90 ·

TRUE OR FALSE:
THE ELECTRIC CHAIR WAS
INVENTED BY A DENTIST.

True. For people who fear the dentist, this
may not be so hard to believe.

91. TRUE OR FALSE: VIAGRA WAS ORIGINALLY INTENDED TO TREAT HIGH BLOOD PRESSURE.

True. Sometimes, the best discoveries are accidental!

92. TRUE OR FALSE: THOMAS JEFFERSON INVENTED MACARONI AND CHEESE.

False. For some reason, this myth has gained popularity over time, but there is no reason to believe it is true.

93. TRUE OR FALSE: PHOSPHORUS WAS DISCOVERED VIA FERMENTED HUMAN URINE.

True. Phosphorus was accidentally invented by a German alchemist who had been fermenting human urine in an effort to turn it into gold.

94. TRUE OR FALSE: THE WORD "DINOSAUR" WAS COINED BY THE ROMANS AROUND AD 800.

False. The word only dates back to 1841. People had found dinosaur fossils before then, but didn't know what they came from.

95. TRUE OR FALSE: PLAY-DOH WAS ORIGINALLY A WALLPAPER CLEANER.

True. The inventor of Play-Doh saw potential in the putty-based wallpaper cleaner he was using, so he re-created it using nontoxic materials and made it colorful.

96. TRUE OR FALSE: ALFRED NOBEL—FOR WHOM THE NOBEL PEACE PRIZE IS NAMED—INVENTED DYNAMITE.

True. Nobel's scientific pursuits were broad, and not always peaceful.

97. TRUE OR FALSE: THE ARTIFICIAL SWEETENERS SACCHARIN, CYCLAMATE, AND ASPARTAME WERE ALL INVENTED BY MISTAKE AND ONLY DISCOVERED WHEN VARIOUS SCIENTISTS LICKED THEIR FINGERS DURING EXPERIMENTS.

True. Please do not follow their example.

98. TRUE OR FALSE: THE CREATION OF THE POPULAR SOFT DRINK FANTA DATES BACK TO WWI.

False. In fact, Fanta was invented in Nazi Germany. When the US embargo prevented the Germans from importing Coca-Cola, Fanta was developed as an alternative.

99. TRUE OR FALSE: DURING THE COLD WAR, THE CIA RAN LITERAL MIND-CONTROL EXPERIMENTS.

True. The MKUltra program didn't go well, and many of the experiment's subjects went on to gain notoriety for all the wrong reasons. Mobster Whitey Bulger, cult leader Charles Manson, and Unabomber Ted Kaczynski are all alleged to have been a part of the experiments.

100. TRUE OR FALSE: NIKOLA TESLA ONCE ELECTROCUTED AN ELEPHANT TO DEATH TO SPITE THOMAS EDISON.

False. It was the other way around. Edison electrocuted an elephant using the alternating current (AC) electricity preferred by Tesla as a means to demonstrate how "dangerous" it was.

Miscellaneous

History doesn't always fit into neat little boxes. There are politics and war, society and science... and then there's the Greek philosopher who died after covering himself in cow manure. Or the time New England blamed an outbreak of tuberculosis on vampires. Or the time a Persian emperor ordered the sea whipped as punishment. The fringes of history are full of fascinating little stories and facts that defy categorization...but they're sure to titillate you nonetheless.

1. **THE ERFURT LATRINE DISASTER WAS AN INCIDENT IN 1184 IN WHICH 60 GERMAN NOBLES FELL THROUGH THE WOODEN FLOOR OF A BUILDING AND DROWNED IN THE LATRINE CESSPIT BELOW THEM.**

2. **NAPOLEON BONAPARTE WASN'T ACTUALLY SHORT.**

Most believe he stood about 5'6", which would have been the average height for a Frenchman during his time.

3. **THE MOST PROLIFIC FEMALE SERIAL KILLER IN HISTORY MAY HAVE BEEN A HUNGARIAN NOBLE NAMED ELIZABETH BÁTHORY.**

As many as 650 murders were attributed to her—though some historians have cast doubt on her guilt over the years.

4. **JUNKO TABEI WAS THE FIRST WOMAN TO SUMMIT MOUNT EVEREST AND THE FIRST WOMAN TO COMPLETE THE "SEVEN SUMMITS" (CLIMBING THE TALLEST MOUNTAIN ON EACH CONTINENT).**

5. **WRITER MORGAN ROBERTSON WROTE A BOOK ABOUT AN ENORMOUS BRITISH OCEAN LINER CALLED THE *TITAN* THAT SANK WHEN IT HIT AN ICEBERG.**

In the book, most of the *Titan*'s passengers died because the ship did not have enough lifeboats. That might sound derivative...but the book was actually written 14 years before the fateful voyage of the *Titanic*.

6. WHEN HALLEY'S COMET WAS VISIBLE IN THE SKY IN 1835, MARK TWAIN WAS BORN.

In 1910, the next time it passed by the Earth, he died.

7. IN THE YEAR 46 BC, JULIUS CAESAR ADDED TWO "LEAP MONTHS" TO THE CALENDAR, WHICH EXTENDED THE LENGTH OF THE YEAR TO AN ASTONISHING 445 DAYS.

8. DURING HIS PILGRIMAGE TO MECCA IN 1324, MANSA MUSA (CONSIDERED THE RICHEST MAN TO HAVE EVER LIVED, WITH HIS ASSETS ESTIMATED TO BE IN EXCESS OF $400 BILLION IN TODAY'S MONEY) STOPPED IN CAIRO, WHERE HE GAVE AWAY SO MUCH WEALTH THAT IT DEVALUED GOLD IN THE REGION AND DAMAGED THE EGYPTIAN ECONOMY FOR YEARS.

9. THE TYRANNOSAURUS REX LIVED CLOSER TO THE TIME OF HUMANS THAN TO THE TIME OF THE STEGOSAURUS.

10. THE LAST LIVING MEMBER OF NAPOLEON BONAPARTE'S AMERICAN DESCENDANTS DIED TRIPPING OVER A DOG LEASH HIS WIFE WAS HOLDING IN CENTRAL PARK, NEW YORK.

· 11 ·

BUZZ ALDRIN MAY NOT HAVE BEEN THE FIRST HUMAN TO SET FOOT ON THE MOON, BUT HE WAS THE FIRST HUMAN TO PEE ON THE MOON.

• 12 •

FREDRIC BAUR, THE INVENTOR OF PRINGLES, HAD HIS ASHES BURIED INSIDE A PRINGLES CAN.

13. IN 1985, ROBERT BALLARD SET OUT TO FIND THE WRECKAGE OF THE *TITANIC*—BUT THAT STORY WAS JUST A COVER.

In reality, his mission was to find the remains of two nuclear submarines that sank in the 1960s. Fortunately for him (and *Titanic* enthusiasts everywhere), he was able to find the remains of the *Titanic* as well.

14. KHUTULUN, THE GREAT-GREAT-GRANDDAUGHTER OF LEGENDARY CONQUEROR GENGHIS KHAN, PROPOSED A CHALLENGE FOR HER MARRIAGE: SHE WOULD MARRY ANY MAN WHO COULD BEST HER IN A WRESTLING MATCH.

If they lost, they would have to give her a horse. Legend says Khutulun won over 10,000 horses.

15. THE US MILITARY ACCIDENTALLY DROPPED TWO NUCLEAR BOMBS ON NORTH CAROLINA IN 1961.

The bombs fell after a B-52 bomber exploded—but fortunately for everyone involved, neither bomb detonated.

16. GRAHAM CRACKERS WERE ORIGINALLY CREATED BY SYLVESTER GRAHAM, A LEADER IN THE TEMPERANCE MOVEMENT WHO BELIEVED IN AVOIDING PLEASURABLE ACTIVITIES.

The crackers were meant to be flavorless and unenjoyable to eat...but somehow they caught on anyway.

17. NINTENDO, KNOWN PRIMARILY FOR PRODUCING VIDEO GAMES, IS MORE THAN 130 YEARS OLD.

It was founded in 1889!

18. IN 1919, 21 BOSTONIANS WERE KILLED WHEN A STORAGE TANK FILLED WITH 2.3 MILLION GALLONS OF MOLASSES BURST, SENDING A WAVE OF MOLASSES THROUGH THE STREETS AT AN ESTIMATED 35 MPH.

19. LONDON HAS ITS OWN VERSION OF THE MOLASSES FLOOD: IN 1814, A FERMENTATION TANK AT THE HORSE SHOE BREWERY BROKE, RELEASING AN ESTIMATED 300,000 GALLONS OF BEER INTO THE STREETS AND KILLING AT LEAST 8 PEOPLE.

20. THE UNITED STATES BOUGHT ALASKA FROM RUSSIA FOR JUST $7.2 MILLION. EVEN ADJUSTED FOR INFLATION, THAT'S JUST NORTH OF $150 MILLION—A PALTRY SUM FOR SUCH A LARGE EXPANSE OF LAND.

21. GREEK PHILOSOPHER HERACLITUS DIED AFTER COVERING HIMSELF IN COW MANURE IN A FAILED ATTEMPT TO CURE HIMSELF OF DROPSY.

· 22 ·

ONE OF THE MOST PROLIFIC PIRATES IN HISTORY WAS A WOMAN.

At the height of her power in the early 1800s, Zheng Yi Sao commanded more than 400 ships and as many as 60,000 pirates in the South China Sea.

• 23 •

THE SANDWICH WAS INVENTED BY (AND NAMED FOR) THE EARL OF SANDWICH IN 1762.

While the story may be apocryphal, the Earl is believed to have wanted a food he could hold in one hand while playing cards.

24. TARRARE WAS A FRENCH SOLDIER IN THE 1700S WHO SUFFERED FROM A TERRIBLE CONDITION: NO MATTER HOW MUCH HE ATE, HE ALWAYS FELT AS THOUGH HE WERE STARVING.

He ate compulsively, and there is evidence that he may once have even eaten a human baby.

25. NOTORIOUS KILLER H. H. HOLMES BUILT AN ELABORATE, MAZELIKE HOUSE THAT HE USED TO ENTRAP HIS VICTIMS AROUND THE TIME OF THE 1893 CHICAGO WORLD'S FAIR.

He used multiple contractors so no one would know the full layout of the house, which he then used to murder at least 27 people.

26. IN 1859, A HOMELESS ECCENTRIC NAMED JOSHUA NORTON DECLARED HIMSELF "EMPEROR OF AMERICA."

The claim was nonsensical, but Norton became so beloved by San Francisco locals that his royal "decrees" were widely published, and he was even permitted to issue his own money, which many establishments accepted.

27. WILLIAM BUCKLAND WAS A BRITISH SCIENTIST WHO LOVED EATING STRANGE AND EXOTIC FOODS.

His strangest meal? Buckland allegedly consumed part of the mummified heart of King Louis XIV.

28. THE *NIÑA*, THE *PINTA*, AND THE *SANTA MARIA* WEREN'T THE ACTUAL NAMES OF COLUMBUS'S SHIPS.

While the *Santa Maria* is probably accurate, the real name of the *Niña* was the *Santa Clara*, and the original name of the *Pinta* has been lost to history.

29. THE PONZI SCHEME IS NAMED AFTER A REAL PERSON.

Charles Ponzi was one of the first to engage in this particular type of scam, and was so successful that it came to be named after him.

30. THE "NEW ENGLAND VAMPIRE PANIC" WAS A TIME IN THE EARLY 1800S WHEN NEW ENGLANDERS BLAMED AN OUTBREAK OF TUBERCULOSIS ON (YOU GUESSED IT) VAMPIRES.

31. TWO OF THE SEVEN WONDERS OF THE ANCIENT WORLD WERE BUILT BY WOMEN: THE HANGING GARDENS OF BABYLON WERE PLANTED BY THE ASSYRIAN QUEEN SEMIRAMIS AND ARE SOMETIMES CALLED THE HANGING GARDENS OF SEMIRAMIS; AND THE MAUSOLEUM OF HALICARNASSUS, THE TOMB OF MAUSOLUS, WAS BUILT BY HIS SISTER (AND WIFE—ICK!), ARTEMISIA II.

· 32 ·

FAMED POET LORD BYRON
WAS SO MAD THAT TRINITY
COLLEGE DID NOT ALLOW
DOGS ON CAMPUS DURING
HIS TIME THERE THAT HE
BROUGHT A BEAR WITH
HIM INSTEAD.

33. WHEN YOU CONSIDER THE AVERAGE NUMBER OF LIPSTICKS PURCHASED OVER A LIFETIME AND THEIR AVERAGE WEARABILITY, WOMEN LICK OFF OR EAT WITH FOOD APPROXIMATELY FOUR LBS. OF LIPSTICK IN THEIR LIFETIME.

This equates to 533.76 lipsticks.

34. ZENG JINLIAN, FROM CHINA, WAS THE TALLEST WOMAN IN RECORDED HISTORY.

She stood an astonishing 8' 1¾"s tall. That's over a foot taller than Shaquille O'Neal.

35. WHEN JULIUS CAESAR WAS 25, HE WAS KIDNAPPED BY PIRATES.

He told them they should ask for a higher ransom, and when it was paid he immediately raised an army, rounded up the pirates, and had them all crucified.

36. JOHN WILKES BOOTH'S BROTHER ONCE SAVED THE LIFE OF ABRAHAM LINCOLN'S SON.

37. ISRAEL IS NOT THE ONLY OFFICIALLY JEWISH JURISDICTION IN THE WORLD; THE JEWISH AUTONOMOUS OBLAST IS AN AREA IN EASTERN RUSSIA ON THE BORDER OF CHINA THAT WAS DESIGNATED FOR JEWISH SETTLEMENT IN 1928 AND STILL EXISTS TODAY.

38. WHEN KING GUSTAV II ADOLPH OF SWEDEN DIED IN 1632, HIS WIFE, MARIA ELEONORA, KEPT HIS HEART IN A GOLDEN CASKET WHICH SHE SUSPENDED OVER HER BED.

39. IN 1579, ENGLISH PIRATES CAPTURED A SPANISH SHIP FILLED WITH CACAO BEANS.

Unfortunately, most Europeans didn't know what chocolate was at the time, so the pirates assumed the beans were animal droppings and burned the ship.

40. IN THE SUMMER OF 1858, THE COMBINATION OF UNTREATED HUMAN AND INDUSTRIAL WASTE POLLUTING THE RIVER THAMES LED TO OUTBREAKS OF CHOLERA AND OTHER DISEASES IN LONDON.

The event, somewhat hilariously, has become known as "The Great Stink."

41. THE US GOVERNMENT ONCE EXPLORED A PLAN TO DEMORALIZE THE SOVIETS BY AIR-DROPPING EXTRA-LARGE CONDOMS INTO SOVIET COUNTRIES IN PACKAGES LABELED "MEDIUM."

· 42 ·

IN 1518, A "DANCING PLAGUE" BROKE OUT IN THE VILLAGE OF STRASBOURG.

Hundreds of people began dancing and refused to stop for weeks, and dozens of people may have died from exhaustion. It is believed to be one of the earliest documented cases of mass hysteria.

43. HEROSTRATUS WAS AN ARSONIST IN ANCIENT GREECE WHO BURNED DOWN THE SECOND TEMPLE OF ARTEMIS IN 356 BC. ASKED WHY HE HAD DONE IT, HE SAID HE SIMPLY WANTED HIS NAME TO BE REMEMBERED THROUGH HISTORY.

I guess it worked?

44. WHEN HE WAS JUST 16, BENJAMIN FRANKLIN POSED AS A WIDOW NAMED "SILENCE DOGOOD" TO WRITE A SERIES OF LETTERS TO THE LOCAL NEWSPAPER.

The persona was so convincing that "Silence" received multiple marriage proposals.

45. PERSIAN RULER XERXES I ONCE ORDERED THE SEA TO BE WHIPPED 300 TIMES AS "PUNISHMENT" FOR DESTROYING HIS PONTOON BRIDGES DURING PERSIA'S INVASION OF GREECE.

46. CHARLES LIGHTOLLER, THE MAN IN CHARGE OF LOADING THE LIFEBOATS ON THE *TITANIC*, LATER WENT ON TO SAVE 130 BRITISH SOLDIERS, USING HIS PERSONAL YACHT, DURING THE EVACUATION OF DUNKIRK.

47. MADAGASCAR IS THE FOURTH-LARGEST ISLAND IN THE WORLD, BUT IT TOOK HUMANS A SHOCKINGLY LONG TIME TO SETTLE THERE.

The first human activity on the island dates back to just AD 500.

48. THOMAS JEFFERSON WAS STILL ALIVE WHEN HARRIET TUBMAN WAS BORN.

When she died, Ronald Reagan had just been born.

49. JOHN TYLER WAS AMERICA'S 10TH PRESIDENT.

At the time of this writing, he still has a living grandson.

50. NAPOLEON'S PENIS WAS STOLEN BY THE DOCTOR WHO PERFORMED HIS AUTOPSY, AND HAS BEEN OWNED BY A NUMBER OF DIFFERENT PRIVATE COLLECTORS THROUGHOUT HISTORY.

51. ANCIENT EGYPTIAN WOMEN HAD EQUAL RIGHTS TO THE THRONE.

While men had higher social status in ancient Egyptian civilization, women enjoyed many of the same legal rights, and were largely viewed as equals in the eyes of the law. Not only that, but the family line in ancient Egypt derived from the mother's side, not the father's.

52. A NAZI CULT LEADER ONCE MURDERED SANTA CLAUS.

In the 1960s, Paul Schäfer staged the (mock) killing of a man dressed as Santa on his Chilean compound, to cement himself as the only figure of worship and adoration for the children in his cult.

· 53 ·

IN THE 1850S, THE CITY OF
CHICAGO WAS SINKING INTO
THE MUD—SO ENGINEERS
RAISED THE ENTIRE CITY BY
SEVERAL FEET OVER THE
COURSE OF A DECADE.

· 54 ·

IN THE MID-1800S, A MAN NAMED EDWARD JONES SUCCESSFULLY BROKE INTO BUCKINGHAM PALACE AND STOLE THE QUEEN'S UNDERWEAR.

He broke in three more times over the next few years, and, unable to keep him out, the British government eventually shipped him to Australia.

55. IN 1913, ADOLF HITLER, JOSEPH STALIN, LEON TROTSKY, JOSIP BROZ TITO, AND SIGMUND FREUD ALL LIVED IN THE SAME NEIGHBORHOOD IN VIENNA, AUSTRIA.

56. IN 1971, A MAN KNOWN ONLY AS "D. B. COOPER" HIJACKED A PLANE, COLLECTED A $200,000 RANSOM, AND PARACHUTED INTO THE WASHINGTON WILDERNESS.

He was never seen again, and to this day no one knows who he was.

57. AFTER SERVING AS A UNION GENERAL IN THE CIVIL WAR, AUGUST WILLICH BECAME A DEVOUT COMMUNIST—SO DEVOUT, IN FACT, THAT HE BELIEVED KARL MARX WAS "TOO CONSERVATIVE" AND CHALLENGED HIM TO A DUEL.

58. BEER IS THOUGHT TO HAVE BEEN INVENTED BY THE SUMERIANS AROUND 8000 BC, IN WHAT IS NOW IRAQ.

Ancient tablets that have been unearthed reveal that the original brewers were women.

59. IN 1666, THE GREAT FIRE OF LONDON BURNED DOWN ALMOST THE ENTIRE CITY...BUT, REMARKABLY, THERE WERE ONLY SIX CONFIRMED DEATHS.

60. TO THIS DAY, MIAMI IS THE ONLY MAJOR US CITY FOUNDED BY A WOMAN.

Julia Tuttle has a statue erected in her honor at Bayfront Park.

61. IN 1841, THE POPULATION OF IRELAND WAS OVER 8 MILLION.

By 1901, a combination of factors, including the Irish Potato Famine, had cut that nearly in half, reducing it to just over 4 million.

62. IN AD 452, POPE LEO I TRAVELED TO MEET WITH ATTILA THE HUN, AND SOMEHOW CONVINCED THE GREAT WARLORD TO END HIS INVASION OF ITALY AND LEAVE PEACEFULLY.

63. ONE OF THE MOST SUCCESSFUL (AND PRODIGIOUS) RACEHORSES IN HISTORY IS NAMED "POTOOOOOOOO."

Pronounced "Potatoes," the horse supposedly got its name when a stable boy who didn't know how to spell potatoes simply wrote "Pot" followed by eight Os.

64. WHEN OSAMA BIN LADEN WAS KILLED BY US FORCES IN 2011, HIS HARD DRIVE WAS RECOVERED AND FOUND TO CONTAIN A SUBSTANTIAL COLLECTION OF VIDEO GAMES, DISNEY FILMS...AND PORNOGRAPHY.

· 65 ·

IN 1855, A RIOT BROKE
OUT ON THE STREETS
OF TORONTO, CANADA,
BECAUSE A GROUP OF CIRCUS
CLOWNS ATTEMPTED TO
USE A BROTHEL THAT LOCAL
FIREFIGHTERS CONSIDERED
TO BE "THEIR TURF."

• 66 •

DRUG LORD PABLO ESCOBAR IMPORTED HIPPOS TO COLOMBIA IN THE 1970S.

After his death, they bred out of control, and a sizable population of hippos exists in Colombia to this day.

67. NAPOLEON HAD A THING FOR BODY ODOR, AND ONCE TOLD HIS WIFE NOT TO WASH, AS HE WOULD BE HOME IN THREE DAYS.

68. A BLIZZARD ONCE KILLED MORE THAN 4,000 PEOPLE IN IRAN.

The 1972 storm lasted nearly a week and dropped as much as 26 feet of snow on parts of the country.

69. THE SECRET SERVICE AGENT WHO SAVED RONALD REAGAN'S LIFE WAS INSPIRED TO BECOME AN AGENT BY THE MOVIE *CODE OF THE SECRET SERVICE*, IN WHICH THE PRESIDENT'S LIFE IS SAVED BY A HEROIC SECRET SERVICE AGENT PLAYED BY...RONALD REAGAN.

70. IN 2019, PEPSICO SUED FOUR INDIAN FARMERS FOR GROWING POTATOES.

Specifically, they were growing the type of potato that PepsiCo uses to make Lay's potato chips, for which the company owns a patent. (The lawsuit was withdrawn after public backlash.)

71. THE UNITED STATES BRIEFLY HAD A 49-STAR FLAG. WHILE THE 48-STAR AND 50-STAR FLAGS ARE WIDELY RECOGNIZED, MOST PEOPLE ARE UNAWARE THAT A 49-STAR FLAG FLEW FROM JULY 4, 1959, TO JULY 3, 1960.

72. *WONDER WOMAN* (2017) WAS THE FIRST SUPERHERO FILM STARRING A FEMALE LEAD TO BE DIRECTED BY A WOMAN.

73. IN 2008, AN ECONOMIC CRISIS IN ZIMBABWE LED TO RUNAWAY HYPERINFLATION THAT PEAKED AT AN ESTIMATED 89.7 SEXTILLION PERCENT.

One US dollar was equal to roughly $2,621,984,228 Zimbabwean dollars.

74. PRESIDENT JOHN F. KENNEDY WASN'T THE ONLY NOTABLE PERSON TO DIE ON NOVEMBER 22, 1963: C. S. LEWIS, AUTHOR OF *THE CHRONICLES OF NARNIA*, AND ALDOUS HUXLEY, AUTHOR OF *BRAVE NEW WORLD*, DIED THAT SAME DAY.

75. FOLLOWING THE UNJUST EXECUTION OF HER HUSBAND, FRENCH NOBLEWOMAN JEANNE DE CLISSON FORMED A PIRATE FLEET AND SPENT MORE THAN A DECADE ATTACKING THE TERRITORY OF THE DUKE WHO WAS RESPONSIBLE.

She was known for leaving a single survivor from each battle to spread word of who she was and why she was attacking.

76. ON HER BIRTHDAY ON OCTOBER 24, 1901, A 63-YEAR-OLD SCHOOLTEACHER NAMED ANNIE EDSON TAYLOR BECAME THE FIRST PERSON TO SUCCESSFULLY TAKE THE PLUNGE OVER NIAGARA FALLS IN A BARREL.

She claimed she was in her 40s.

• 77 •

WHILE JOAN OF ARC
WAS CHARGED WITH MANY
CRIMES, THE ONE THAT WAS
USED TO HAVE HER BURNED
AT THE STAKE...WAS HER
REFUSAL TO STOP DRESSING
AS A MAN.

78. AN ESTIMATED 10-15 MILLION PEOPLE DIED IN THE BELGIAN CONGO DURING THE BRUTAL REIGN OF KING LEOPOLD II—NEARLY HALF THE POPULATION OF THE REGION.

79. 9/11 WAS NOT THE FIRST TIME A LARGE AIRCRAFT STRUCK A NEW YORK CITY BUILDING; IN 1945, A B-25 BOMBER FLEW DIRECTLY INTO THE EMPIRE STATE BUILDING AMID HEAVY FOG, KILLING 14 PEOPLE.

80. BETWEEN 1999 AND 2006, CONSERVATIONISTS HUNTED DOWN AND KILLED EVERY SINGLE GOAT ON THE GALAPAGOS ISLANDS.

The goats had bred so prolifically that they were inflicting tremendous damage on the unique vegetation of the islands.

81. TRUE OR FALSE: HISTORIANS CONSIDER KING TUT TO HAVE BEEN THE MOST POWERFUL EGYPTIAN PHARAOH.

False. King Tut wasn't a particularly important pharaoh. In fact, the main reason we know of him today is because his was one of very few pharaoh tombs that hadn't been desecrated by grave robbers by the time it was discovered.

82. TRUE OR FALSE: BY LOSS OF LIFE, THE *TITANIC* WAS THE SINGLE BIGGEST MARITIME DISASTER IN HISTORY.

False. Not even close. In 1945, the MV *Wilhelm Gustloff* sank while carrying almost 10,000 German civilians and military personnel fleeing the encroaching Red Army. The death toll is estimated at around 9,000.

83. TRUE OR FALSE: BENJAMIN FRANKLIN AND ISAAC NEWTON WERE ALIVE AT THE SAME TIME.

True. Newton lived until 1727—not quite long enough to see the American Revolution, but long enough for Benjamin Franklin to be born in 1706.

84. TRUE OR FALSE: THE GREAT WALL OF CHINA IS THE ONLY MAN-MADE OBJECT VISIBLE FROM SPACE.

False. The Great Wall doesn't actually stand out much. It can be seen from low orbit under specific conditions, but the same could be said for numerous other man-made objects.

85. TRUE OR FALSE: ANNE FRANK, BARBARA WALTERS, AND MARTIN LUTHER KING JR. WERE ALL BORN IN THE SAME YEAR.

True. It sounds fake, but they were all born in 1929. It's just that we associate them with three very different periods in history.

86. TRUE OR FALSE: THE CHILDREN'S SONG "RING AROUND THE ROSIE" IS ACTUALLY ABOUT THE BUBONIC PLAGUE.

False. This is a popular myth, but it's just one in a long list of children's songs for which people love to invent dark backstories.

87. TRUE OR FALSE: THE INFAMOUS GENERAL CUSTER FINISHED DEAD LAST IN HIS CLASS AT WEST POINT.

True. It certainly didn't stop him from rising up the ranks.

· 88 ·

TRUE OR FALSE: THE 1900 OLYMPICS FEATURED "POODLE CLIPPING" AS AN EVENT.

False. This false fact has traveled far and wide, but actually originates in a 2008 April Fools' Day article published in *The Daily Telegraph*.

• 89 •

TRUE OR FALSE: CLEOPATRA LIVED CLOSER TO THE TIME OF THE MOON LANDING THAN TO THE TIME OF THE BUILDING OF THE PYRAMIDS.

True. This one isn't just a rumor. By the time Cleopatra ruled in Egypt, the pyramids were already ancient.

90. TRUE OR FALSE: JOHNNY APPLESEED WAS A REAL PERSON.

True. His name wasn't Johnny Appleseed, but John Chapman did spread apple seeds across a significant portion of the United States and Canada.

91. TRUE OR FALSE: IN 1895, THE ONLY TWO CARS IN THE STATE OF OHIO CRASHED INTO EACH OTHER.

False. This is a popular myth, but there isn't any evidence that it actually happened.

92. TRUE OR FALSE: MARCO POLO WAS JUST 17 YEARS OLD WHEN HE BEGAN HIS FAMOUS JOURNEY.

True. He didn't set out on his own, but still. Impressive!

93. TRUE OR FALSE: THE FIRST DRIVER TO RECEIVE A SPEEDING TICKET WAS ALSO THE FIRST DRIVER TO EXCEED 100 MPH IN A CIVILIAN VEHICLE.

False. The first speeding ticket in world history was issued in 1896 to a driver going 8 MPH. To be fair, that was four times the speed limit at the time.

94. TRUE OR FALSE: FAMOUS PHILOSOPHER VOLTAIRE USED TO RUN THE FRENCH LOTTERY.

False. In fact, he cheated the lottery! Voltaire initially became wealthy by using basic math to game France's flawed lottery system.

95. TRUE OR FALSE: HITLER'S FAMILY DOCTOR WAS JEWISH.

True. And Hitler personally intervened to protect him during the Holocaust.

96. TRUE OR FALSE: THE NAME "IDAHO" MEANS "GEM OF THE MOUNTAINS."

False. Idaho means...absolutely nothing. The man who suggested it was a con artist who claimed it was a Native American word. It was not.

97. TRUE OR FALSE: HENRY FORD ONCE TRIED TO BUILD AN ENTIRE FACTORY TOWN IN THE MIDDLE OF THE AMAZON RAIN FOREST.

True. He called the failed experiment "Fordlândia," and its ruins can still be found there today.

98. TRUE OR FALSE: WHEN THE GREAT PYRAMIDS WERE BUILT, WOOLLY MAMMOTHS STILL ROAMED PARTS OF THE EARTH.

True. It's always fascinating to think about what was going on in different areas of the globe.

99. TRUE OR FALSE: CATHERINE THE GREAT DIED WHILE ATTEMPTING TO ENGAGE IN INTERCOURSE WITH A HORSE.

False. This rumor is believed to have been started by Catherine's enemies, who sought to undermine her reputation and influence even after her death.

· 100 ·

**TRUE OR FALSE:
ALEXANDER THE
GREAT ONCE HOSTED A
WINE-DRINKING CONTEST
THAT CAUSED 41
CONTESTANTS TO DIE OF
ALCOHOL POISONING.**

True. No one can accuse Alexander the
Great of throwing a boring party.

[Acknowledgments]